App...
boo...
(new...

pp. 10-11, 12-13, 26-27, 30-31,
42-43, 46-47, 58-59, 62-63,
74-75, 78-99, 94-95, 106-10
110-111, 138-139
122-123, 126-127

note for Twitty p. 61

# HISTORICAL  SKETCH
## OF  BOOKBINDING
### AS  AN  ART

# HISTORICAL SKETCH
# OF BOOKBINDING
# AS AN ART

BY

MEIRIC K. DUTTON

NORWOOD

THE HOLLISTON MILLS, INC.

1926

This Book
is respectfully dedicated and distributed by
THE HOLLISTON MILLS, INCORPORATED

TO

AMERICAN BOOKBINDERS

# CONTENTS

# HISTORICAL SKETCH
## OF BOOKBINDING
### AS AN ART

# CHAPTER I

## BEGINNINGS OF BINDING

THE HISTORY of the art of bookbinding is always parallel to the history of artistic taste in every country. It has flourished with every movement for the advancement of art and has fallen with every materialistic revolution. Its decadence has been evidence of a decadence in the manners and morals of the times; its rise has been a barometer of the increasing affluence and well-being of a country and a people.

The earliest records of bookbinding carry us back at least to the sixteenth century before the Christian era. In the Assyrian collection of the British Museum, there is preserved a set of terra cotta tablets of this date. They were each taken from covers of the same material. These covers, on each of which was impressed a title similar to that on the enclosed tablet, were broken in order to reach the contents.

Tamil manuscripts and certain manuscripts from Japan are also given a very early date. Narrow strips of palm leaf uniform in size make up the pages of these manuscripts, which are protected by flat pieces of wood or carved ivory and bound tightly together. In the British Museum is a Tamil manuscript with

3

a rounded back produced by using large sheets at the center and gradually reducing the width of those added at either side. By jogging to the fore-edge a circle is formed at the back which is tightly fastened by a surrounding metal band. This manuscript successfully incorporates the principle of our modern rounded books except that the front is flush instead of following the curve of the back.

The early Greek and Roman books were written on long skins or strips of parchment or vellum sewn together and rolled on one or two cylinders of wood, reed, metal or ivory. The leaves, after being trimmed and squared, were polished on the outside with pumice. The rolling of the volume (*volumen*) around this cylinder completed the binding except for the ornamentation of the knobs and the attaching of the title, inscribed on vellum or parchment, near the top of the roll. A sprinkling of cedrium, an oil for preserving the vellum from decay and insects, was usually added.

Catullus gives a description of this method of binding in discussing a poet named Suffenus. A translation of the discourse follows:

> *His paper is royal, not common or bad,*
> *His wrappers, his bosses, are totally new;*
> *His sheets, smoothed by pumice, are all ruled with lead,*
> *And bound with a ribbon of rose-colored hue.*

This method of bookmaking was not entirely abandoned until the sixteenth century, a beautifully il-

4

luminated roll of prayers with miniatures of the end
of the fifteenth century being preserved in the Archi-
episcopal Museum at Utrecht. The more precious
of these *volumina* were enclosed in wrappers of
leather and canvas, and then placed in wooden
cases.

The Roman *pugillaria,* or table books, formed a
step between the scrolls and modern binding. They
were composed of from two to eight leaves of ivory,
wood or metal connected at the back by rings, and
covered with wax on which the impression of the
stylus was made. The covers were at first made
of parchment or other skin and later of boards.

Thomas Frognall Dibdin, in the Eighth Dialogue
of his *Bibliographical Decameron,* claims the ancient
*diptych* to be the real precursor of modern binding.
These were larger than the *pugillaria* and consisted
of two covers of ivory, ebony or boxwood which protected the work within, the whole being held together
by two or more hinges. These *diptychs* contained
the acts of consuls and other public officers. The ornaments on the cover were often done in carved ivory,
gold or precious stones, though many of them were
without decoration.

At about the beginning of the Christian era the
adoption, by both Greeks and Romans, of something
like a desk brought with it the use of square or oblong
sheets for the work of transcribing. The date at
which this change took place cannot be exactly deter-
mined; nor can we tell at just what period the Athe-

5

nian, Phillatius, to whom the Greeks erected a statue, discovered glue, a material which hastened the binding of books in the modern fashion. However, it is known that in Cicero's time the use of glue was prevalent, because of the passage in his *Epistles to Atticus* (56 B.C.) in which the orator asks his friend for "some two of his librarians, who, amongst other things, might *conglutinate* his books."

So much authority has been placed on this passage as signifying the existence of a library of books in the modern sense of the term, that it may be well to quote the section at length: "Etiam velim mihi mittas de tuis librariolis duos aliquos, quibus Tyrannio utatur *glutinatoribus,* ad cetera administris, iisque imperes, ut sumant membranulam ex qua indices fiant, quos vos Graeci, ut opinor, σίλλυβους appellatis."

At all events, it was a natural succession of steps from the writing of oblong sheets to the folding and gathering of sheets in twos and fours, the former denoting a folio shape and the latter a quarto. Upon the discovery of glue, with which these sheets might be held together, the stages of covering and exterior decoration came with little effort.

Suidas in the tenth century gives an interesting confirmation of the use of leather for binding by the ancients when he states that the Golden Fleece, in search of which Jason and his Argonauts went, was but a book which taught the art of making gold. This book, he says, was bound in sheepskin.

6

A contemporary proof comes from the *Notatia Dignitatum Imperii* of about 450 A.D. which mentions that the officers of the Byzantine Empire carried in public ceremonies large square books of the emperor's instructions, bound in red, blue or yellow leather and ornamented with a gilt or painted portrait of the emperor.

Of course, the first natural covers for oblong sheets were oaken boards, — smooth and unadorned. Then, in proportion to the wealth of the owner and the esteem in which he held the manuscript, these boards came to be ornamented in silver, gold and precious stones. Monastic bodies played an important part in the preservation, and later in the ornamentation of books, since most of the manuscripts of early times were of a religious nature. In the fourth century Saint Pachomius, the founder of the first organized monastic community, made it a rule in his monastery that they should work for the preservation of books. As a result of the cloistered origin of books the ornaments often take the form of religious symbols, — the Virgin, the Infant Saviour, and the Crucifixion.

Horace, Cicero, Pliny and other writers, both Greek and Roman, show us that the work of the ancients put the art of bookbinding on something of the high level which it holds today. Yet, as has been intimated in our reference to the *Notatia,* we must look to the progress made in the Byzantine Empire. Byzantine coatings, which were of gold and silver set with precious stones, were introduced in the West as binding ornaments at some time previous to the sixth century.

At this time bookbinding was the art of the goldsmith and enameler, for Seneca, Petrus Acotentus and other philosophers are on record as having criticised the luxurious ornamentation of books. It was with reference to this that Saint Jerome exclaimed, " Your books are covered with precious stones, and Christ died naked before the gate of His temple." These exhortations availed little in the face of the demand for decoration. The *Silver Book of Ulphilas* (370 A.D.) of which descriptions may be found, was an example of this work. It is a book of the Gospels translated by Ulphilas, Bishop of Moesia, and was bound in massive silver. At this period, and until the ninth century, potentates gave specially adorned manuscripts to churches and monasteries as marks of favor.

Early in the sixth century, Belisarius found among the treasures of Gilimer, King of the Vandals, a book of Scriptures "glittering with gold and precious stones." The earliest binding known to have come down to our time is that on a copy of the Greek Scriptures, bound in two plates of gold ornamented with a cross set with stones and cameos. This was given by Theodelinda, Queen of the Lombards, to the Basilica of S. John Baptist at Monza at the end of the sixth century.

A celebrated copy of the *Pandects of Justinian,* in

8

the Laurentian Library of Florence, is of the seventh century. It is in two large folio volumes, bound with wooden boards which are covered with red velvet and ornamented with silver covers. Apparently this work was not known to Dibdin, who wrote, " Of binding in velvet, I take it we have no specimens before the fourteenth century." The binding to which Dibdin here refers may be that covering a copy of *Boccaccio* of, perhaps, the fourteenth century, which is described as being " covered with red velvet, and had on each cover five large rubies."

A somewhat different style of bookbinding was at this time being instituted in the Celtic countries. Of the early books of Ireland little is known, although it is thought that the art was carried on by artisans connected with Saint Patrick (c. 440 A.D.). These craftsmen and their successors found richly ornamented bindings impractical, since the Irish ecclesiastics were often forced to travel many miles afoot through dangerous country in order to reach their various parishes. It was therefore necessary that the books should be as light in weight as possible and that they should not be so ornamented as to prove tempting prey to robbers.

The hardships imposed on the books of the missionaries during their long journeys demanded some further protection than the regular cover. To meet this demand book-satchels were introduced as a part of their equipment. These satchels were of rough leather and were made at least twice the width of

9

the book. The extra leather was gathered in a knot which was fastened under the traveller's girdle. Book-satchels as well as bindings were ordinarily without decoration, but when they were for a man of high repute, they were beautifully ornamented. The satchel of an Irish *Missal* which is now preserved at Corpus Christi College, Oxford, is a rough leather case upon the sides of which is stamped a pattern of intersecting lines and circles produced by a blunt point and punches.

The plain style of Celtic bindings extended to most of the books which were gifts to churches. Since the covers were often the handiwork or at least the gift of the patron saint of that church, the books were kept in their original coverings but were usually placed in beautifully decorated book-shrines. On these boxes or shrines were lavished all the ingenuity of the goldsmith. The earliest known shrine was made for the *Book of Durrow* by Flann Sinna, King of Ireland, late in the ninth century, although it is probable that book-shrines were in use for some time before that date.

Although most of the bindings of the Celts were without decoration, there are extant some examples of beautiful workmanship which show that Celtic binders could skillfully adorn books in leather and metal. Dagaeus, an Irish monk of the sixth century, is said to have employed gold, silver and precious stones in the binding of books. Ethelwulf, in the ninth century, calls to our attention the ingenuity of another early monk, Ultan, in the ornamenting of books. Many fragments of Celtic bindings have been found, including engraved clasps, corner pieces and metal plates.

An example of Irish binding in the early part of the eleventh century is to be found in the cover of the Molaise *Gospels*. This binding is made of bronze plates ornamented with silver and gilt patterns which are riveted to the bronze. Between the arms of a cross appear the four sacred beasts, and gilt cable patterns fill the remaining spaces. Stones are placed at the four corners. The Stowe *Missal* is ornamented with a large rosette of metal in which is centered a crystal. From this crystal extend the arms of the cross. An inscription forms the border. There are also extant some leather bindings executed by Celtic craftsmen, who were adept at designing on this material.

During the period in which the Irish binders were developing their national style, the English monks were busily engaged in pursuit of the craft. Their art follows somewhat more closely that which was being produced on the Continent, but the gradual appearance of individualistic ornamentation laid a foundation for the ensuing English supremacy in bookbinding. In practically every monastery, cloisters were set aside for the transcribing and binding of books. At Winchester and Durham, particularly, we find monastic bodies engaged in bookbinding. In fact, since the monks of the Mediaeval times

were the only people out of hearing of the din of
battle, the entire task of preserving and beautifying
manuscripts fell to them.

Bilfrid, a monk of the Benedictine monastery at
Durham in the early eighth century, is supposed to
have bound the *Textus Sanctus Cuthberti* of which
Astle tells us. It is covered with silver and gold
plates ornamented with precious stones. On it are
depicted the Crucifix, John and Mary. When the
monks of Lindisfarn were fleeing before the dep-
redations of the Danes, the boat in which, with
their belongings, they were huddled, overturned and
this book fell into the sea. Because of the merits
of Saint Cuthbert, the sea receded to such an unusual
degree that the book was found unharmed on the
sands three miles from shore.

Our knowledge of early English books and their
binding is very much limited because of the acts of
the Reformers who caused the destruction of count-
less libraries. Through the cupidity of the lieuten-
ants who executed these acts, many valuable bindings of precious metal were destroyed, whether or
not they contained references to the papal religion.
Some good examples, however, did escape and are
now extant in various English and Continental mu-
seums and libraries. In the library at Stonyhurst
College is a binding in red leather of about the tenth
century. On the upper cover is a raised ornament of
Celtic design, above and below which are panels of
interlaced work colored with yellow paint. The

under cover is decorated with a geometric design picked out in yellow.

Another existing book is the *Passionale,* which was used for the coronation oath of all English kings from Henry I (1100 A.D.) to Edward VI (1547 A.D.). This book is covered with two oaken boards which are nearly an inch thick, the whole being fastened together with thongs of leather. The corners are protected with brass bosses and a gilt-bronze crucifix adorns the top cover.

On the Continent, an Oriental influence was making itself felt in the almost pure Byzantine art which was being followed in the closing years of the sixth century. This tendency is traced by the elongation and the angularity of form as well as by an increasing richness of costume. Artists from Constantinople coming to Italy and Germany doubtless brought with them certain aspects of the art of the East. Gradually the Byzantine style lost its local importance and, with individual variations, became the general form of book decoration throughout Europe.

Early in the ninth century, Emperor Charlemagne attached his name to a style of art. As the result of a dispute which Empress Irene had with bishops concerning images, Charlemagne called a conference of artists at which were represented both the Celtic and Byzantine schools. By this bringing together the East and the West, Charlemagne created a new style of binding which is known as Carolingian.

These ninth century books are noted for their

gorgeous exterior decorations as well as for their exceptional calligraphy. A *Book of the Gospels,* given by Ada, sister of Charlemagne, to the Abbey of Saint Maximinus of Treves, was studded with gems encircling an agate five inches in width and four in length on which were engraved representations of Ada, the Emperor, and his two sons. Though this book is not now extant, it is carefully described by Mabillon in his *Annales.*

Another beautiful binding of this period is of South German workmanship. The cover is for a copy of the *Gospels* and is entirely of gold and jewels. A cross in the center is formed by a structure of openwork in gold. In the center of each compartment of an arched filigree border is a gem or pearl. Four large pearls appear in the inner corners of the cross, with four sapphires at the ends. Thirty-two each of pearls and carbuncles, set alternately, nestle between. A group of jewels set on small lions' feet lodge between the arms of the cross as well as at intervals in the border and at each of the terminations of the cross. Three rows of stones or pearls complete the border of this Carolingian cover.

A twelfth century binding of the *Gospels* in Greek is now in the British Museum. The wooden boards are covered with tarnished red velvet and are lined with a fine canvas, embroidered with silk. Thin plates of silver-gilt with figures in relief which are nailed to the upper cover are probably of the tenth century. The plates along the top and bottom of the cover contain half length pictures of Saint Peter, Saint Paul and the four Evangelists. Plates along the sides depict the overthrow of the heresiarchs Nestor and Nestus in three designs. The center plate is of a much later date.

Another twelfth century binding of excellence is that covering a Latin *Psalter*. This binding was executed for Melissenda, daughter of Baldwin, King of Jerusalem. Inserted in the wooden covers and surrounded by a binding of red morocco are two ivory carvings of a somewhat earlier date. Six scenes from the life of David are shown enclosed in circles on the upper cover. The figures in the intervening spaces symbolize the triumph of the Virtues over the Vices. The cover represents in the six circles the works of Mercy surrounded by figures of birds and beasts. Both covers are jeweled with small rubies and turquoises. Depressions in the ivory at the fore edge of the book indicate that clasps were fastened to it, though they have been lost.

The close of the Carolingian period was marked by the introduction of the art of enameling on book-covers. Although this art existed in certain sections of Western Europe as early as the third century, the practice was neglected along with every other art during the wars of the succeeding centuries. While the West was occupied with invasions, the East was developing all branches of art, and it was through Constantinople that enameling found its way back to Europe early in the eleventh century. At this time, Emperor St. Henry secured some Greek artists to adorn the covers of his books of prayers in enamel.

There were several methods of enameling, two of which are very important. The first is termed *cloisonné* from the fact that the vitreous compounds of various colors were embedded in designs or compartments which were first outlined by fine strips of metal soldered in relief upon a ground of metal. This method was customarily employed by Greek and Italian artists. The second method is known as *champlevé* and was used by the artists of Limoges. The designs of Limoges enamels were cut into the metal and the cavities thus formed were then filled in with enamel. Into this latter class fall most of the enameled bindings which are now extant.

The Cluny Museum in Paris boasts of two Limoges enameled book covers. One of these represents the adoration of the Magi while the other depicts the monk Etienne de Muret and St. Nicholas. An interesting example of *cloisonné* enamel is preserved in the National Library in Paris and is of Byzantine workmanship. It is composed of four minute enamels which form a flower. Opaque white and light blue are used with semi-translucent green. The library at Munich harbors a binding of the eleventh century containing medallions executed in *cloisonné* enamel.

Some examples of enameled bindings are found also in American collections. The library of Robert Hoe contained several such works, including some of

16

early Persian execution and several of Italian and Flemish workmanship which bear somewhat later dates. A Byzantine plaque for a book cover is of particular note, being worked in bronze which is gilt and enameled.

Translucent enamels were later introduced in book covers by Italian artists because of the need of a less clumsy medium. These enamels were placed directly over engravings in gold or silver. The engravings show plainly through the colors. Few specimens of this work have been preserved, partly because of the great value of the metal which proved tempting to thieves and to some extent because the thin enamel was brittle and chipped off. *Historic Bindings in the Bodleian Library,* by W. Salt Brassington, describes an example of this work which covers a thirteenth century copy of a Latin *Psalter*. Each side is made of a silver plate enameled with deep and brilliant translucent colors. The enamels represent the Coronation of the Blessed Virgin and the Annunciation.

Velvet as a binding material had long been used both in England and on the Continent, as has been pointed out. Its use during the fourteenth century became more prevalent than at any preceding time. These bindings were ornamented with clasps and bosses of gold and often bore a plaque in the center containing the arms of the prince or nobleman for whom they were made.

During the period in which the Continental binders were perfecting enamel plaques for book covers,

English artists were reaching their supremacy in stamped leather bindings. Cities and monasteries throughout the country competed for the highest honors in this field. It is now practically impossible to determine the heights to which the English attained in binding books in precious metals and gems, since a great number of these examples have doubtless been destroyed through religious intolerance coupled with the cupidity of thieves. It is only through the efforts of Mr. W. H. James Weale that any account of the English stamped leather bindings of the twelfth and thirteenth centuries has been pieced together, since they fared only slightly better than the more elaborate bindings.

To the monks of the Benedictine Monastery at Durham and other similar organizations goes much of the credit for the English advance in the art. Strength and durability were originally the aims of the monastic binders. The sheets were sewed on strips of skin or parchment, and often each sheet was further protected with a strip of parchment as a guard to protect the back from injury and to prevent the thread from cutting through the sheets. Forrell-bindings, or bindings in oaken boards covered with roughly dressed deer-skin, superseded the unadorned wooden covers. Some instances are known of books bound in this manner with the hair left on the leather.

The dressing and ornamenting of leather bindings followed gradually. A tenth century binding of the

*Gospel of St. John* is extant, showing interlaced ornaments impressed on dark crimson leather. The use of punches and tools gradually increased in England until, in the twelfth century, small stamps appeared which, it is claimed, have "never been surpassed for beauty of design and execution." These stamps were cut in intaglio, which gives an impression resembling a cameo, the effectiveness of these stamps depending on high lights and shadows.

The stamps were arranged in formal designs either in segments of circles or as parallelograms, and varied in every cover decorated. In many instances, the character of the design differs on the upper and lower, being arranged in a rectangle on one side and in circles and semicircles on the other. Birds, beasts, fish and flower designs are carried out on some stamps, while on still more are pictured knights, bishops, angels and various fantastic animals.

A famous binding in this style is the one covering the *Bible* done by the Benedictine monks of Durham for Hugh Pudsey, bishop of that See, and which he later gave to the Cathedral Library where it is now preserved together with other of his books. The *Bible* is in four volumes on the bindings of which fifty-one stamps are impressed, twenty-seven different ones being used on the first volume alone.

A copy of the *Liber Sapientiae,* bound at Durham, which is now in the British Museum, is of the late twelfth or early thirteenth century. Small square dies of varying design form the borders of this binding, within which appear stamps in horizontal and vertical lines depicting birds, beasts and other characters.

Although much of the English claim to supremacy may well rest on the work of these monks of Durham, there were also some excellent craftsmen at Winchester, London and other cities who substantiate the claim. The *Winchester Domesday Book* which is preserved in the library of the Society of Antiquaries was made in Winchester in 1148. This binding contains eleven different stamps. The center of the upper cover carries ten impressions of a rectangular stamp, placed in two vertical rows. A double border is formed of oblong stamps with an arched stamp connecting the outer border at the head. The under cover is made in the pattern of two roses.

An example attributed to London workmen of the thirteenth century is now extant in the British Museum collection. A border is formed on each side by the repetition of stamps. Eight oblong stamps form the back border of the obverse cover. Dragons with interlaced tails are depicted on these. Ten square stamps of a foliated ornament appear near the fore-edge, palmated leaves connecting them. These borders enclose eight impressions of a stamp bearing a lion passant. Circular and lobe-shaped stamps are also employed. A binding from York which is now in the Bodleian Library at Oxford contains at least thirty different stamps arranged in the formal manner of this style. Rosettes and lozenge-shaped interlacings are also introduced and at the corners are palmated leaves pointing outwards.

The invention of printing and the subsequent flooding of the country with foreign books caused the downfall of the English supremacy in bookbinding. Certain it is that all the national characteristics in the art which had been so laboriously acquired had vanished by the end of the fifteenth century. At this time many foreign binders came to England, bringing with them stamps which they had employed on the Continent.

The two centuries immediately preceding the discovery of printing witness a great advance in bookbinding in nearly every country. In Germany, the art of ornamenting leather was making great progress by the use of the *cuir bouilli* method. The leather was cut slightly, outlining the desired figure or ornament, and then raised a trifle in relief. This method was started as early as the ninth century, but the fourteenth century brought the introduction of a punched surface to the background, which was sunk slightly, leaving the design in relief.

The designs, which are of fabulous and grotesque animals and twining foliage, display great freedom and spirit. The variety and artistic merit of these bindings, which were entirely executed by hand, together with the richness of the decoration, display the German art at its height. At no time since has Germany achieved a national style of binding.

France had already distinguished herself during

the Carolingian period, and until shortly after the invention of printing was satisfied to follow in the wake of her neighbors. Although the customary materials were used in the binding of books, they were left without decoration or were finished to receive plaques of ivory and metal.

The few ornamented leather bindings of this period show an English influence. One binding, which is said to have been executed in the thirteenth century for St. Louis, is covered in a red pigskin parchment and is stamped with the fleur-de-lis and the towers of Castile, which was the emblem of Louis' queen. The stamps are arranged in vertical rows in accordance with the English fashion of the time. From the inventories of the possessions of noblemen of this time it may be seen that most of their books were covered in velvets, brocaded silks and other stuffs.

The advances made by Italy during the fourteenth and fifteenth centuries is particularly notable. The city of Siena is noted for its collection, which probably extends from the thirteenth to the seventeenth century. The painted covers of the Treasury books of this city have been framed and hung in order in the corridors of the Palazzo del Governo.

Italian artisans were famed for their leather bindings. As in the countries already discussed, the monks played an important part in this development in which the technique of the Orient was closely followed. In spite of a variety of stamps the work executed in the monasteries was invariably dull and lacking in spirit, although technically good. During the thirteenth century, however, the work was taken up by craftsmen who were connected with the universities and a more free and impassioned spirit is immediately discernible.

From the thirteenth century, the number of books in circulation was greatly augmented each day. With the increase in the number of books came also a broadening of the interests of readers, and the contents of the volumes dealt with a more varied list of subjects. The fact that the great universities had connected with their organizations a number of writers, illuminators and binders at once changed the tone of the contents, and the collectors demanded bindings which were in accord with the ideas of the text. Great princes and noblemen secured the services of binders and had their own ideas executed.

Books, therefore, took on a more gay aspect both interior and exterior as soon as the craft was partially freed from the fetters of the monastery. By the end of the fourteenth century a notable change was apparent even in the bindings of the monasteries. The designs became more fluent. Compartments were sometimes stained in colors and other changes may be noted.

Since it is from the bindings of the Italian monks that the most beautiful bindings of the Renaissance are descended, it would be a gross injustice to forget or ignore their art. The amateurs and followers of bookbinding did not deviate from the technique of the monks, but they allowed their designs to be influenced more by the tastes and customs of the time.

The introduction of metal dies brought with it a remarkable improvement, since it permitted hot stamping, which process gives a greater clearness to the cameos and intricate designs than the old cold stamps. They also increased production and could be alternated and combined into many patterns. Some of these combinations in the libraries of kings and collectors of the fourteenth to the sixteenth century show an extraordinary development in the artistic taste of book decoration.

Throughout this period, great strides were being made in the art of forwarding books, although the final advances were not made until the sixteenth century. It is difficult to understand how these bindings with great metal bosses and clasps, or books entirely encased in silver *repoussé*, were arranged on bookshelves until it is realized that they were kept on lecterns in the churches for which they were made or were laid flat on shelves in the library of the individual owner. As may be gathered from the consistent use of ties or clasps until the sixteenth century, the edges of the vellum pages cockle and gape at the fore-edge unless they are strongly restrained. The early printed books also display this tendency as a result of the too heavy impression given by printers of that period.

24

Another peculiarity to be noted in manuscripts as well as early printed books is that the backs of the bindings never received any of the lavish decoration which was bestowed on the recto and verso of the books. This also is attributable to the gaping of the leaves at the front. Books which were not protected by bosses or clasps could be stacked in piles, but the fore-edge was so much greater in thickness than the back that they had to be piled with their backs to the wall, as otherwise the top books would be at so great an angle that they would fall to the floor.

It was necessary, therefore, to find some other method of designation than the one so common to us today. Vellum bindings were often made so that an enveloping flap on which the title of the book was written came over the front edge. Other books are found to have had the title simply written across the edges of the leaves. To this peculiarity may also be ascribed the beautifully gauffered fore-edges of this time. In *The Binding of Books*, by Herbert P. Horne, is pictured the back of a book dated 1534 of which he says: "The title is lettered, not only upon the upper lid, but, also, upon the back of the book. This is one of the earliest instances of the back bearing the title of a work, although Le Roux de Lincy notices that some of Grolier's books are thus stamped with his name."

In the fifteenth century, the materials for covers and the style of their preparation had greatly advanced the art of binding. The scattering of the libraries of the Byzantine Emperors at the fall of Constantinople had spread much information throughout the circle of the craft and the subsequent flight of many of the binders of the East to Florence, Venice and other Italian cities aided collectors in their seeking for artists to produce beautiful covers.

The introduction of printing at just this time is supposed to have saved many of the classics from a loss which, through the slightest accident, might have occurred at any moment. The classics were for the most part issued from the presses of the early printers immediately after the invention of printing. With the rapid rise of printing, a similar demand for bookbinders arose.

Bookbinding is greatly indebted to the patronage of the wealthy lovers of books and it is largely through their collections that the art must be traced. Although little is known of his library, Mathias Corvinus, King of Hungary from 1457 to 1490, may lay claim to the title of FATHER OF BOOK COLLECTORS, to which honor Grolier is often appointed because of the great quantity of his books still extant. Corvinus came to the throne but one year after the printing of the first book, the Gutenberg Bible, to which is given the date of 1456.

Three libraries are said to have been founded by him in Buda, one of which reached great prominence. His books, which are variously numbered between 30,000 and 50,000, consisted chiefly of manuscripts bound in brocade and protected by bosses and clasps

26

of silver and other precious metals, although many were in stamped leather and red velvet. Most of his books carry his device, which was a black crow with a ring in its mouth. Thirty scribes and illuminators at Buda and four scribes at Florence, by the courtesy of Lorenzo de' Medici, are said to have been continuously in his employ. Almost the entire library was destroyed by the Turkish soldiers in the siege of Buda in 1526.

In Italy the artists in bookbinding found encouragement and aid in the Medici family. Piero de' Medici, of the middle of the fifteenth century, is the earliest of the family known to have been interested in this field. Gildings, miniatures and other decorations ornament the manuscripts which he collected and which he distinguished by his mark, the fleur-de-lis. Later in the same century, Lorenzo de' Medici continued this interest.

In Western Europe, Philip the Good, Duke of Burgundy, kept a constant stream of authors, scribes and illuminators. Louis de Bruges, Seigneur de la Gruthuyse, employed artists in Bruges and Ghent to write and bind his books; and Henry VI of England is still remembered for his encouragement of literature as well as for the books bound for him which are now in the Royal Collection of the British Museum. The Duke of Bedford and Humfrey, Duke of Gloucester, are also to be listed among famous collectors of this period.

The issuing of books in such numbers as was possible after the invention of printing necessarily brought about a change in the methods of binding which, from this time, fall into two distinct classes: trade bindings and private bindings. The early printers, excepting possibly Aldus, appear to have issued their books in sheets which were subsequently bound by the stationer or for the collector himself. It may readily be seen that these bindings, being produced much more rapidly, lost much of their individuality, although they did retain a certain distinction of national style.

Some of the more interesting private bindings of this period were executed in silver. A late fourteenth century silver binding in the British Museum has on its upper cover a brass figure of Christ sitting on a throne with, at the four corners, sprays of leaves set each with a precious stone. The border is of silver plates crudely joined together, at the corners of which are tablets of gold and black enamel with the emblems of the four Evangelists. The lower cover is much the same in character, but the design is somewhat better since there are no interfering stones or tablets.

The Bodleian Library boasts an early eighteenth century silver binding of extreme purity to which has been added the further embellishment of an ivory plaque of the eleventh century. The ivory represents the Saviour seated upon a richly carved throne.

In America, we find the library of Robert Hoe to

have housed some perfect examples of silver-gilt bindings in *repoussé*. One covering a manuscript *Book of Hours* carries biblical scenes on the backstrip as well as on the two covers and with engraved borders is of seventeenth century Flemish work. Another seventeenth century Flemish or German binding is of blue, black and gold enamel set in silver filigree. A beautiful example of open work silver over black stamped seal-skin is of the eighteenth century.

Still another silver binding in the Hoe Library demands attention as well for the sanguinary scenes it depicts as for its magnificence. This seventeenth or eighteenth century binding has on its covers two *repoussé* designs of incidents in Judges. One shows Adoni-bezek, King of Canaan, having his thumbs and great toes cut off, and the other pictures the killing of Sisera with Jael standing, hammer in hand, and her victim nailed by his head to the threshold. Flowers and ornaments appear outside the beaded borders of these scenes. The back contains four scenes in as many panels, all from Joshua. The hanging of the five kings, Joshua commanding the sun and moon to stand still, Rahab letting down spies from the town wall and the ark compassing the city of Jericho, are here represented. Such detail in silver bindings must overshadow the importance of other private bindings in brocades and velvets.

On a sixteenth century binding in purple velvet which was done for Queen Catherine Parr, the embroidery is worked on linen and the tracery is a couching of gold cord. A shield is worked in a variety of intricate stitches while the crown is in solid gold and decorated with raised gold work of pearl and gold cord. An embroidered binding from the library of Queen Elizabeth pictures a rose tree in bloom and four deer.

To come again to the library of Robert Hoe, there is an old Dutch binding, probably of the seventeenth century, of purple silk, which employs not only colored silk and gold threads in its embroidery, but groups of pearls as well are introduced in the design. Bindings of this style, however, are rarely to be found outside of the great national libraries of Europe.

In the trade bindings of this period, the most important step was made in the Netherlands, where the panel stamp was invented about the middle of the fourteenth century. By this method, the entire side of a book could be stamped from one block at one impression. The Netherlandish designs were unusually formal, the center panel bearing spirals of foliage in which were introduced fabulous animals and birds. A motto is often found around the edge with the binder's name or initials.

The stamped bindings of the French are more often in a pictorial pattern. Jehan Norris used a stamp showing the vision of Emperor Augustus and another of Saint Bernard. Stamps portraying Christ, the implements of the Passion and the saints were also used. The binders of Rouen and Caen were influenced by the English work of the period because of their traffic in English service books, which were often bound as well as printed in France.

Foreign craftsmen flooded England with the invention of printing, and destroyed the former fame of English stamped bindings which had become a distinct national style. William Caxton, returning to England in 1477, brought with him the tools and the methods which he had used in Bruges. Using leather for the covering material he ruled the sides in diagonal lines. These diamond-shaped compartments were stamped with designs of flowers and fantastic beasts.

The bindings of Germany continued to depict fabulous animals in twining foliage. The designs were carefully cut in outline with a sharp knife and the background was peeled away. The figures were then engraved and the depressed portions stippled. Brass corner-pieces with raised bosses to protect the leather from injury were used. Borders of intersecting fillets generally appear, and between these fillets and the edge of the book, diamond- and almond-shaped stamps are impressed.

Italian bindings of the end of the fifteenth century are particularly interesting for their variety. One in the British Museum has in the center of each cover an embossed medallion. Each medallion is enclosed in a green border and this is surrounded by a triple border in blind tooling. Interlaced ornamental work appears between each of the sets of border rules.

Rings washed in gold as well as red and gold roundels are inserted in the cover.

Another interesting Italian binding of the end of the fifteenth century has on each cover a border and panel of interlaced cable-work tooled in blind. It is in work of this design that Italian decorators were to introduce gold tooling into Europe.

## CHAPTER II

## BINDING IN ITALY

GOLD TOOLING was first introduced into Italy at the end of the fifteenth century. Although the exact date and manner of the introduction of this art are uncertain, it is known that it came from the East, where it is said to have flourished in Syria as early as the thirteenth century. Both Germany and Italy claim the credit of having first employed this art. Certain it is that traces of gold are found on some of the bindings of Anton Korberger of Nuremberg early in the last quarter of the fifteenth century, but the gold appears to have been painted on instead of being applied by the impression of stamps.

In Italy, both Florence and Venice claim the distinction of having first used gold tooling. Vittorio de Toldo in *L'Art Italien de la Relieur du Livre* assures us that "in all probability the binders of Florence were the first who thought to enrich the fronts and backs of books with impressions in gold." To support this claim he cites that the Duke Hercules d'Este had volumes in his library with Florentine bindings decorated in this manner.

By far the greater number of authorities give the honor to Venice, believing that the knowledge was acquired by the Venetians in the course of their trade

33

with the East rather than that it was brought to Italy by some of the Greeks who fled to that country after the fall of Constantinople in 1453. At all events, the first general application of the art was made by Aldus Manutius, the renowned Venetian printer and binder, although occasional single examples have been found bearing slightly earlier dates.

For forty years after his birth in 1450, Aldus was devoted to education and teaching. It was not, therefore, until about 1494 that he became sufficiently imbued with the ambition of spreading learning by means of the printed book to establish his press; and his binding operations did not begin until some time later with the appearance of his Latin classics in 1501.

In these classics, Aldus represented the book for the first time as an instrument of daily work which could be handled with ease. The forwarding of books had at this time improved to such an extent that on the small volumes which were issued from this press, it was no longer necessary to use clasps except in extraordinary cases.

An innovation directly attributable to Aldus is the replacing of the wooden boards by pasteboard, at once making for easier handling of books and reducing the danger of bookworms, with which the wooden covers were infested. It was in his workshop also that books were first produced without raised bands on the back. This innovation was probably made at the suggestion of the Greek workmen

34

in his shop, who had learned their trade in Persia where this practice was common.

Owing probably to the influence of these same workmen, as well as to the fact that the entire art originated in the Orient, the tools which were used show unmistakable signs of Eastern origin. The interlaced or Arabic work which appears in the knots and borders of his bindings are also reproduced in the decoration of the initials in the books themselves. The earliest Aldine tools were solid, being similar to those used in the printing of the text. But it is in the use of the tools that Aldus excelled, having always in mind the " knowing economy " which was employed by all the great artists of the Renaissance.

Joseph Cundall in *Bookbindings: Ancient and Modern* calls to our attention the use of the Aldine anchor in " numerous books which, it may be presumed, Aldus bound for the library of Grolier." On this very subject, however, Herbert P. Horne discourses at some length in connection with a description of an Aldine binding from his own library. This book, a copy of the *Statius* of 1502, is in its original binding. The covers are decorated by a figured border in blind, of arabesques ending in dolphins, formed by the repetition of a single tool: and in the center of the panel, enclosed by this border, is a knot of Arabic work in gold tooling. The back has double bands and the edges are gilt and gauffered. This book also possessed two clasps on the fore-edge. In questioning the reference of the dolphin, Mr.

Horne says, "The question remains whether the dolphins, occurring in the border of this binding, were used in allusion to the Aldine mark of the Dolphin and the Anchor, which M. Gruel, repeating, perhaps, the assertion of MM. Marius Michel, states to be found upon some bindings of Aldus. Such an example, I have not had the good fortune to see."

Of the early bindings of Aldus few are still in existence. The British Museum exhibits a copy of the *Sonnets of Petrarch* of 1501 in its original cover of dark olive green morocco which is typical of the earlier work of this shop. Particular care has been exercised in the decoration of this volume since the copy is printed upon vellum. A series of knots and Aldine leaves ornament the covers and are surrounded by a double border, one of which is figured and the other knotted. These ornaments are entirely in gold tooling while the back is richly tooled in blind. The edges of the boards, which are of wood, are grooved according to the peculiar manner of the Italian binders of this period.

Filippo di Giunta, the Florentine printer who early copied the italic type of Aldus, seems also to have imitated the bindings of the Venetian artists. Copies of the *Divina Commedia* of Dante and of the *Commentaries* of Caesar which are now in the British Museum have on their bindings leaves and knots of Arabic work in gold and blind tooling. The recurrence of the same tool on these bindings makes

36

it appear that Giunta had these very binders working for him in his own shop.

Other instances of the repetition of the same tools in the bindings of various printers, however, make it difficult to determine with any certainty just which, if any, of these printers had their own staff of binders. An explanation for this recurrence has been offered to the effect that Aldus employed gilders whom he found already in Venice, and that he allowed them to use their own tools with the addition of certain others for his own particular use. A defect in this explanation appears in that the dolphin, which may be considered essentially an Aldine ornament, has been found on bindings from other workshops. All these difficulties make it impossible to speak with any certainty regarding the binders of this period and the bindings from their shops.

The bindings of the early Aldine period are marked by the use of a few simple tools which are used sparingly and in such a manner as to produce a richness which has never been excelled.

Although, as has been said, the bindings of the early Aldine period are of such beauty that they were never excelled in their class of ornamentation, yet the house of Aldus was still to produce another style which is far more noted and perhaps more beautiful.

This new style is directly attributable to the influence of Jean Grolier, who became associated with Aldus as his patron about the year 1512. Dibdin remarks that it is almost a waste of time and words to discuss the great influence of Grolier on the bibliopegistic art. However, it is necessary to include some discussion of the bindings executed for him, although his patronage has been so often and so ably related.

Jean Grolier, Vicomte d'Aguisy, was born at Lyons in 1479. The office of Treasurer of the Duchy of Milan descended to him from his father in 1510 and in 1516 he married Anne Briconnet. In 1534 Grolier was sent as ambassador to Pope Clement VII. He obtained the reversion of the office of Treasurer-General of France in 1545 and was installed in this position in 1547, holding the post until his death, at Paris, October 22, 1565.

Beginning with the year 1520, bindings for Grolier which were undoubtedly of Aldine execution appear with the interlaced geometrical designs. These interlacings have greatly added to the fame of patron and craftsman alike. There is scarcely one large collection of books which does not include at least one typical example of these Grolier bindings.

M. Le Roux de Lincy gives, under the title *Recherches sur Jean Grolier, sur sa Vie et sa Bibliothèque*, a catalogue of 355 books from the library of this collector. These books are principally Greek and Latin classics and most of them bear the Aldine device. While this catalogue is a monumental work for the study of Grolier's library, many examples have been found which apparently were unknown to de Lincy. It is estimated that this catalogue contains but one-tenth of his original collection.

The first Grolier bindings were of the interlaced strapwork arranged in geometrical patterns as has been said. In a plaque high in the center of the recto appears the title of the book and at the foot a panel bearing the words IO. GROLIERII ET AMICORVM. Of this phrase Dibdin says: " You will understand from the subjoined inscription that he wished his books to be used by his friends as well as by himself. Grolier is the first who set the memorable example of liberality."

While it is never necessary to question the spirit or the style of Dibdin, it here appears again that the veracity of his statements may be questioned. Certain it is that Tommaso Maioli used the inscription THO. MAIOLI ET AMICORVM, but in this case we cannot be at all sure of the dates, since practically the only fact known of him is that he was still living in 1555. Yet no less an authority than Joseph Cundall says that Grolier imitated Maioli in the use of the inscription. At about this same period Io. Chevignardi, Renati Thevenyn and Marcus Laurinus also used the motto. Charles and Mary Elton incline to the belief that the phrase had its origin in a letter written by Philelpho, in which he tells his correspondent of the Greek proverb that all things are common among friends.

The reference that the books belong to his friends as well as to himself may be interpreted to mean that he was free in the lending of his books or, more probably, that he had duplicate copies of many books which he gave to his friends. The catalogue of de Lincy notes no less than five copies of the *Virgil* of 1527 from the Aldine press and four copies each of the *Hypnerotomachia* of 1499 and of *Juvenal* of 1501.

The existing examples of Grolier's bindings show that almost invariably a motto was placed on them, generally on the verso. Early in his association with books, we find on the bindings an emblem consisting of a hand issuing from a cloud, trying to pull an iron bar from the summit of a mountain, and upon the garter which surmounts the emblem appears the motto, AEQVE DIFFICVLTER (The golden mean is hard). This emblem is supposed to depict some hardship under which Grolier labored.

With approaching success, this phrase gave way to the words of the Psalmist, PORTIO MEA DOMINE SIT IN TERRA VIVENTIVM (Let my portion, O Lord, be in the land of the living). Grolier varied this legend by the use of TANQVAM VENTVS EST VITA MEA as well as CVSTODIT DOMINVS OMNES DILIGENTER SE, ET OMNES. Sometimes his arms — azure, three bezants or, in point, with three stars argent in chief — are used.

From the first stage of stiff geometric designs Grolier's bindings soon become more fluent by varying the straight lines with graceful semicircles. These bindings, which usually hold copies of the Latin and Italian classics printed with the italic types of Aldus,

are covered either with mottled brown calf or with
morocco of a reddish-brown or olive-green color.
The nature of the leather is not easily detected because of the smooth surface to which it is worked.

The guarding of these books in their covers marks
another advance in the forwarding of books. A section at the front and end of each volume is formed of
a sheet of vellum between two sheets of paper which
are folded once and sewn with the rest of the book.
The outer leaf of paper is pasted to the board, together with one of the vellum leaves, thus forming
a joint of vellum and leaving three fly-leaves of paper
and one of vellum.

The British Museum holds at least thirty copies
from the library of Grolier, many of them being in
the collection bequeathed to the Museum by the Rev.
Clayton Mordaunt Cracherode in 1799. Mr. Cracherode formed a wonderful library, partly from his
ability to take advantage of the sales of valuable
books at the time of the French Revolution. A
Grolier binding from this collection is in a reddish-
brown morocco, having the sides decorated in a geometrical design with scrollwork. The recto is entirely unlettered except for Grolier's friendly motto
at the foot. On the verso, which is decorated in the
same manner, appears his favorite passage from
Psalm CXLII. This is one of the few Grolier books
without bands on the back. In the absence of this
decoration, it is ornamented with a fish-scale pattern.

Another Grolier presented to the Museum by Mr.

Cracherode is in citron morocco with the interlaced geometrical design of double fillets on each side. Inside this design is a panel formed of ornamental tooling, these tools being of typical Aldine form and weight. The name of the author appears in the center panel of the recto, the verso containing Grolier's legend. At the foot of the recto are the words IO. GROLIERII ET AMICORVM. On the back of this book appear five bands upon which the signatures are sewn, and two kettlestitch bands, tooled with lines in blind and gold. The edges are plain gilt. This is the style of back and edges found on most of the treasurer's books.

The design of these bindings is entirely of geometric origin, although in some instances the small Aldine stamps are introduced. Later we find attempts to join these two elements into the basic design. In Grolier's bindings this attempted union is attended with but little success. In view, however, of the many varied efforts made by him, the failures are singularly few.

Of this type Vittorio de Toldo reproduces several examples in his *L'Art Italien de la Reliure du Livre*. The decoration of one of these consists of what appear to be vines intertwined in scrolls, each of the vines ending in a leaf. In the center is left a circular plaque on which is inscribed the title of the book. Both the scrolls and vines are done in outline so the general effect of his earlier binding holds, although the beauty is lessened by the burden of decoration.

Another binding shows a combination of an irregular geometric pattern together with solid stamps. In this case the arabesques have no relation either in position or in weight to the remainder of the design.

While in Venice Grolier also seems to have had executed for him several bindings in which the strapwork of the geometric design and the flowers were in gold and then painted in black, green, red and other colors. While these imitation mosaics undoubtedly were striking at the time of their execution, the paint has been chipped or become dulled so that there is now but little attraction to them.

Grolier will, of course, be longest remembered as a result of the use of morocco and gold tooling on his bindings. His was the first great collection on which these materials were used, and the typical Grolier binding will remain the interlaced strapwork of geometric designs either with very few or no flowers.

Tommaso Maioli forms a figure of interest to booklovers second only to Grolier; and it is not at all incomprehensible that his bindings should be considered by many as superior to those of the French Treasurer.

Dibdin raises the lament that he is absolutely ignorant of the personal history of this great amateur, and that cry must still be passed down, although it now appears that Mr. G. D. Hobson, the English authority, may have a solution in his claim that the name is Mahieu, becoming Maiolus when Latinized. Practically no record of his existence can be found except that story which is told by his collection of books. It is not known where he was born, where he lived or where he died. It is supposed that he may have been a relative, possibly a nephew, of Lorenzo Maioli of Genoa, one of the earliest Italian collectors, and an author of considerable learning, Aldus having published two works written by him in 1497. This uncle was also a professor of philosophy at Ferrara.

It has also been contended in a tract, *Maioli et sa Famille*, by M. Aimé Vingtrinier, that Maioli may be a Latinized form of Mayol, the name of a Provençal house of St. Mayol. Certain tendencies in his bindings which will be discussed seem to give credence to this contention. These same tendencies also favor Mr. Hobson's claim.

Ample proof has been forwarded to support the claim that Maioli enjoyed the companionship of Grolier. Joseph Cundall in *Bookbinding: Ancient and Modern* calls our attention to a book in the possession of M. Brunet which bears Maioli's name stamped on the cover, while upon the title page Grolier's famous motto, PORTIO MEA DOMINE SIT IN TERRA VIVENTIVM, is written in his own hand. This is undoubtedly the copy of a translation of the *Psalms* into Italian which Herbert P. Horne mentions in *The Binding of Books*. This copy is now in the Public Library at Lyons, where may also be found a copy of the *Offices* of Cicero which has

44

Maioli's stamp and in which Grolier has written his name.

From the dates appearing on other books bound for Maioli, we may judge that he started his career of collecting in about 1530 and that he was still living in 1555. After that date no trace can be found of the bibliophile. It may even be advanced from the information now current that Maioli lived at a slightly earlier period than Grolier. However, certain refinements in his bindings seem to discourage this theory, although some few authorities incline to its belief.

Certainly the bindings of Maioli are more beautiful in the spontaneous freedom of their curved lines and arabesques and the harmonious combination of these decorations with the curved strapwork than are those of Grolier. In most of the bindings of Grolier, the geometric lines form the entire pattern and any other ornaments have the appearance of being an afterthought and consequently do not harmonize with the main design. In Maioli's bindings, the flowing scrollwork, the graceful curves which interlace freely with the subordinate framework give a movement to the design. It is here again that the bindings of Maioli gain a depth that escapes the design of Grolier.

These characteristics have been described as the difference between the more florid style of Italy which Maioli retained and which Grolier allowed to become affected by the severity of the French. On the books of Grolier the framework is the design itself, being a

45

geometric composition of interlaced straight lines
and semicircles. The ornaments, although similar
in character to those of Maioli, are not as advan-
tageously placed and do not blend with the scrollwork, but are worked in without due regard for the
perfection of curve.

The framework of Maioli's bindings is less the
design than is the scrollwork and is made up of curves
rather than of geometric patterns. The ornaments
of each are Moresque in character, those of Maioli
being either in outline or azured, while those of
Grolier were azured or solid. Maioli very effectively
dotted certain enclosed sections of his pattern in gold,
which, together with the slender sprays of conventional foliage, added richness and elegance to otherwise formal designs. He often placed scrolls and
foliage in white edged with gold on a dark background of leather.

Although the historical facts of the life of Maioli
are almost entirely lacking, we are most fortunate
in that a great number of his bindings have been preserved and examples are now to be found in nearly
all great collections, both private and public.

On one side of his books is generally to be found
his liberal motto, THO. MAIOLI ET AMICORVM, although this may be found in connection with a monogram of the initials A.E.H.I.L.M.O.P.S.T. In M.
Guigard's *Nouvel Armorial du Bibliophile,* an authority without peer on the subject, these initials are
made to form the name E. P. Thomas Maioli, but

this solution is unsatisfactory since an N and an R, instead of a P, appear in this cypher. Moreover, the name at length invariably accompanies the symbol and this would seem needless repetition. It, therefore, probably stands as an abbreviation for a legend. The motto INIMICI MEI MEA MIHI NON ME MIHI, which may be read freely, " My enemies are able to take mine from me, not me from myself," also figures on many of his bindings.

In the British Museum is the *Hypnerotomachia* from the library of Maioli. It is bound in dark olive morocco having each cover ornamented with an arabesque border which is variously stained black, studded with gold dots or left plain. The ornaments are both solid and azured. On the upper cover this border encloses a panel of light olive colored morocco which is inlaid. In the center is a cartouch bearing the title of the book. The panel on the lower cover contains a cartouch which is not inlaid as is that on the upper cover, and here is displayed the disputed cypher. The back is without bands, being decorated with arabesque tooling.

Pictured in Boerner's *Bucheinbände Katalog XXI* is an *Exemplaria Literarium* bound for Maioli, which is of great beauty. It is bound in black calfskin with compartments composed of straight and curved fillets about which arabesques have been interlaced in a flowing pattern. The covers are richly decorated, carrying a base of gold points in a central tablet which also contained a monogram.

47

The library of Robert Hoe contained several fine copies of Maioli's books. A copy of *Fregulphi Episcopi* is bound in brown calf. The ornamentation is entirely of curved fillets, into the design of which have been worked arabesques in outline. The design is enclosed in a frame border and entirely covers the board except for an oval in the center which carries the title. The legend THO. MAIOLI ET AMICORVM appears at the foot of the upper cover.

Another beautiful binding from this source is that covering a *Procopius de Bello Persico* in brown calf. The decoration of this is composed of flowing scrollwork, the compartments of which are painted black, red and white, while gold dots form a background for certain enclosures. A little plaque at the top and bottom of each cover is decorated with solid and outlined arabesques and a central cartouch on the upper cover contains the title, while that on the lower cover contains a monogram. Maioli's name appears at the foot of the upper cover. Another copy in this collection carries the motto INIMICI MEI MIHI NON ME MIHI.

The facts that scarcely any of Maioli's bindings have raised bands on the backs and that there is a certain firmness of line in the scrollwork may seem to indicate a slight French influence which Maioli may have acquired at home, provided, as claimed, that he was of a Provençal house. However, it is more safe to assume that these influences were acquired in the channels of trade and that Maioli's bindings

48

were executed in Venice and that he was a Venetian, at least by adoption.

Foreign influence is most markedly discernible in the so-called " Venetian " bindings. The craftsmen of this school obtained their style directly from the Persian and Arabian manuscripts with the result that the appearance is decidedly oriental.

Examples of " Venetian " bindings found on copies of the *Commissioni Ducali* and the *Investiture Ducali* bear evidence that the school was favored by the Doge as well as by the Senate. This kind of binding was begun in Italy about the beginning of the sixteenth century, reaching its height about fifty years later.

The board was coated with a paper composition and the center and corners were then cut out in the desired shapes. Then the entire board, both the recessed panels and the upper ground, was covered with a thinly pared leather which took the form of the cut-out recesses. This leather was then coated with a colored lacquer and lastly decorated and painted with arabesques in gold.

The vogue of such a distinctly oriental style is easily explained by the close political, intellectual and commercial relations that existed between Venice and Greece, Asia Minor and Persia, which connections made Venice a veritable corner of the Orient. Artists of all classes copied without stint from the examples displayed by the Levantine merchants. Having admired the rich merchandise of the East,

49

it was but a step to the imitation of its wares. The
bindings of the Arabian and Persian manuscripts,
which were resplendent in gold, mosaics, colors and
lacquers, fairly cried to be reproduced.

In this manner, the Venetian craftsmen adapted
the style of oriental binding in which the morocco is
worked openly and superimposed in its depths with
colored skins. For some time after its introduction,
the craftsmen were so imbued with the spirit of the
Orient, that their compositions were faithful to the
originals, the style of which was comprised of a depressed oval centerpiece altered into the shape of a
double bow, decorated in the interior with flowers
or ornaments in color on a gold base, with quarter
sections of this same ornament — or one very similar
— in each of the corners, and sunken panels with
a similar treatment as a border.

However, this type of decoration proved so flexible
as to admit almost limitless ostentation in the application of gold, colors and mosaics and the "Venetian" bindings of the end of the century displayed
a "corruption in the taste." Here again an excellent
style was ruined by a lack of that "knowing economy" for which the Renaissance had become justly
famed.

One "Venetian" binding of the second half of the
sixteenth century which is preserved in the British
Museum is in red morocco, with sunken panels decorated with Oriental designs stamped in slight relief
on a gold base.

Another binding in this style is also in red morocco, with compartments ornamented in colors on a base of gold in the Arabian manner. It carries on its front board the lion of St. Mark painted in relief on gold; the back board is similarly decorated with a coat of arms. In the border, ornaments are painted in colors over gold.

The South Kensington Museum, London, owns a collection of stamps and tools used by craftsmen in producing bindings of this style.

Cameo bindings were also prevalent in Italy at this same period, an example of this style having already been presented. Counterpieces of designs in relief, taken usually from antique gems and medals, form the distinguishing feature.

These real cameo bindings must be distinguished from the stamped imitations of certain French binders at a slightly later period. The material of the cameo is a vellum pressed while damp upon the die. Some composition of lacquered paste is put on to the leather to fill up the cavities and preserve the shape of the figures.

Such are the bindings which have become connected with Demetrio Canevari, the physician to Popes Urban VII and VIII. Since the practice of cameo making in this style stopped in 1560 and the date of Canevari's birth is recorded as 1559, it is probable that he inherited his famous library from some older member of his family.

These books bear in the center of each cover an

oval plaque representing Pegasus standing on Mount Helicon, with Apollo driving a chariot with two horses over the sea towards him. The cameo is surrounded by a Greek legend which is translated, "Straight forward and not obliquely." The dies from which this design is stamped vary according to the size of the book on which it is used. On large volumes, the greater diameter of the oval is set upright; on small volumes, lengthways.

In these cameos, the figure of Apollo was painted flesh color, his helmet, robe and the body of the chariot being gilt. One of the horses is painted white, the other black. Pegasus is covered in silver, as are the clouds and wheels of the chariot.

A copy of *Polydore Vergil* in the British Museum is from this collection. In addition to the title on the front cover, it also appears on the top panel of the back strip. This is supposed to be one of the earliest cases in which the title was lettered on the back.

Other notable Italian bindings of this period appear in the libraries of Apollonio Filareto, Cardinal Bonelli and Marcus Laurinus. The latter was a devotee of the phrase ET AMICORVM, applying it to practically his entire library. He was a scholar, antiquary, collector and friend of Grolier, as evidenced by a book in the library of the Louvre bearing the inscription IO. GROLIERIVS M. LAVRINO, D.D.

Cardinal Bonelli was created a cardinal by Pope Pius V in 1556. The notable volumes from his library are bound in morocco, carrying his coat of arms, name and title of the book, surrounded by decorations of arabesques and geometrical designs.

Apollonio Filareto employs a medallion consisting of an eagle soaring upwards, above rocks and the sea with fish swimming in it; the whole being surrounded by a ribbon with the motto PROCUL ESTE. This medallion is surrounded by an ornamental panel composed of beautiful geometrical and arabesque tooling.

## Chapter III

## BINDING IN FRANCE

To the time of the introduction of gold tooling, it has semed advisable to adhere to a chronological reckoning of the progress of the art of binding in terms of centuries. From this period, however, every art centered about the sovereigns of the various countries and was directly related to the particular taste of a specific monarch. Because of these rapidly changing styles, it is necessary to follow any art in relation to the monarchical régime in effect at the time.

Although there were certain individual collectors who preserved a distinctive style, the general law in artistic taste was set by the sovereign and followed explicitly by his court. Of course, no particular style ended exactly on the day of the death of a king, but a change was very soon effected bringing into play the ideas of the newly appointed ruler.

In France, as in Italy, the bindings of the first printed books differed but slightly from the bindings of the manuscripts immediately preceding. Just as the main output of the scribes was ecclesiastical books and Latin classics, so were the first printed books the writings of Dante, Petrarch and Boccaccio, Books of Hours and Bibles. Consequently the bind-

ings of the early printed books of France which are
found in the Bibliothèque Nationale and the libraries
of Sainte Geneviève and Rouen are ornamented with
monastic stamps, the designs of which MM. Marius
Michel describe in *La Reliure Française* as " seeming when followed with an attentive eye to unroll
under the regard, reduced to the proportion of
jewels."

The library at Troyes also contained many bindings in this style which were taken there for preservation at the time of the revolution from the numerous
convents of Champagne.

The bindings of France were, of course, greatly
influenced and the art was largely advanced by the
Guild of St. Jean Latran which was established in
Paris as early as 1401 by a charter from Charles
VI. The founding and subsequent actions of this
confraternity are elaborately described by M. Ernest
Thoinan in *Les Relieurs Français*. Much of our
knowledge of early French binders is gathered from
records and documents of the Guild which M. Thoinan has collected.

The charter of Charles VI, dated the first of
June, 1401, authorizes Nicolas de Bosc, J. Postié,
H. Marescot, scribes; Jacques Richier, illuminator;
J. Chapon, publisher; Guillaume Deschamps and
Simonet Milon, binders, to found a confraternity
in the Church of Saint André des Arcs, under the
invocation of Saint John the Evangelist. A con-
firmation of this charter was issued in June, 1467,

*" publishing as
an old
profession "*

by Louis XI. The wording of this confirmation discloses the information that the Guild was largely of a religious nature; the celebration of three masses being among the chief obligations.

At the time of the founding the members of the Guild were well-to-do, but the records show that as Paris later became impoverished "by great wars, famines, mortalities and other pestilences," and the numbers of the community decreased, Louis XI was forced to issue a statement increasing the annual dues of the members in order to meet the obligations of the Guild. This edict also stated that the Guild should thereafter be under the protection of the mayor of Paris. Previously the Guild of St. Jean Latran had been under the control of the University and therefore enjoyed privileges not extended to other guilds.

In 1582, an arrangement was made whereby the religious ceremonies of the community should be held in the church in the Quartier de l'Université. Later, in 1618, letters formally authorizing the Guild were secured from the king, approved and enrolled.

In order to acquire membership in the Guild, it was necessary to have been bound apprentice to a master binder in Paris for a term of five years, to have served as journeyman for an additional period of not less than three years, and to have received the recommendation of two free men in the presence of the master and his colleagues.

From the time of the issuing of this edict until

1730 the history of the Guild forms a series of disputes. At this time the separate branches of the community reorganized entirely apart and the binders and gilders retired to the Church of St. Hilaire. In 1776, an attempt was made by Turgot to suppress the city Guilds of Paris but, on his dismissal, they were reorganized, coming to a final dissolution by an act of the Assembly in March, 1791.

The chief value of the records of the Guild to the present-day historian is a complete list of the wardens of the community from the year 1618 through the remainder of its life. Four wardens were in office at any one time, two of these officers being elected every other year.

Of Royal French bindings of the fifteenth century there are but few. Although Charles VIII seems to have been a lover of books, those carrying his arms are extremely rare. After his expedition into Italy, however, he brought back with him from Naples a large portion of the library of the King of Aragon.

Louis XII also seems to have had but few books bound for himself, those bearing his arms being of extreme rarity. Louis was the first to have both his device and motto on his books. Before his marriage to Anne of Brittany, he employed a semis of bees and the motto NON UTITUR ACULEO REGINA CUI PAREMUS. After his marriage he used the monogram L. A., with or without the crown. This was generally used with the arms of France and the ermine of Brittany. The hedgehog, which was his emblem, adorns many of his books together with the motto COMINUS ET EMINUS.

MM. Marius Michel mention a binding in the Bibliothèque Nationale bearing the arms of the King and of Anne of Brittany as well as the hedgehog. A binding in the Bibliothèque Mazarine containing the arms of Louis XII was also bound in France according to this authority.

Following his conquests of Milan, Louis assembled a large part of the libraries of the Visconti and the Sforza in his library at Blois. Here he also placed the library which he bought from the famous amateur Louis de la Gruthuyse of Bruges. It is strange that such a great lover of books should have had so few of his own bindings.

At this period the artistic decoration of books is often accredited to the binder, although, in reality, he often had little or nothing to do with it. In the sixteenth century binding was done in the shops of stationer-booksellers and the stationer receives this credit.

Sometimes the printer was also the binder, but this was the case only when he was a stationer as well. Much of the work done during this period was commercial binding, which means that the books were issued by the printer-binder-stationers decorated by stamps on which the entire ornament was cut. This is distinguished from the hand tooling which was executed for Grolier and other great patrons of the art.

The term "commercial binding" has come to be regarded as a slur on the workmanship and beauty of a volume. This is due to the present fashion for craftsmanship, the followers of this fad believing that anything in which the hand of the worker cannot be definitely traced is of inferior quality.

From the early start in decorating volumes with blind stamping, it soon became associated with gold decoration. M. Léon Gruel in his *Manuel Historique et Bibliographique de l'Amateur de Reliures* traces the use of stamps from the blind stamping period through the introduction of gold ornaments, listing Philippe Pigouchet, Denis Roce, Robert Mace, the Gryphes of Lyons, Christophe Plantin at Antwerp, Jean Bogard, Madeleine Bourselle, Jacques Dupuis and the Elzevirs among the important workers in this art.

During the first half of the sixteenth century, Geoffroy Tory's bindings, with his stamp of the broken pitcher, were produced. This stamp was taken by the famous writer, artist, engraver and printer when he became bookseller. In his *Champfleury,* Tory says that Grolier employed him to design certain letters for him. It has been suggested that these may have been the characters used by Grolier on his bindings and it is also probably that Tory had some share in their decoration.

Two bindings in the so-called Tory style, one in the British Museum and the other in the Bibliothèque Nationale, may have been bound with his stamps some time after his death, which probably occurred in 1533, since we find his business being conducted by his widow in 1534, it being transferred to Oliver Mallard the next year.

Tory, however, is known to have been an excellent binder. For the decoration of his bindings he used stamps forming panels of arabesque which are worked in with borders and other ornaments. These arabesques are imitated in form from the contemporary Italian work which Tory studied while receiving his education in Italy. The manner in which they are designed, however, is peculiar to him. The personality of the original artist is here recognized for the first time in the decoration of bindings.

The British Museum binding referred to is on a volume of *Petrarch* which was printed in Venice in 1575. M. Henri Bouchot describes the binding in the French National Library. Each of these books carry the designer's mark, the broken vase. In the second, the vase is pierced by a *toret* or auger. This device Tory explains in his *Champfleury*. The broken vase represents our body, which is a vessel of clay, and the auger is fate, which pierces both weak and strong alike. The *toret* is also probably a punning device on his name.

Francis I of France was a great patron of the bookbinding art although examples of the work done for him are rare. The characteristics of his bindings become even more definite in those of his successor, Henry II. In these bindings a delicacy and refinement is apparent which later becomes the chief characteristic of the French craftsmen.

The British Museum possesses one example of the work done for Francis I. This book is ornamented with a series of rule borders, at each of the four corners of which is placed a fleur-de-lis. Each cover bears his arms as King of France, surrounded by the Order of St. Michel, and ensigned with the royal crown. Below the arms is a salamander, the device of the king, and on each side is a crowned F.

Other bindings executed for him are decorated in the style of Grolier and still more have a diaper pattern composed of alternating stamps of the crowned F and the fleur-de-lis. Practically all bear the arms of the king and his device, the salamander in flames. His motto, NUTRISCO ET EXTINGUO, also appears on some bindings. The device and motto were given him in childhood by his tutor Boisy.

Etienne Roffet, called Le Faulcheur, and Philippe le Noir are the only two binders claiming the title of *Relieurs Ordinaires du Roi* under Francis I, although it has been suggested that Geoffroy Tory may also have worked for him in designing patterns.

In the books bound for Henry II and his mistress, Diane de Poitiers, some authorities consider that the art of bookbinding in France reached its highest development. Severe simplicity characterizes many of these bindings, the use of tooled ornaments often being limited to their emblems — the interlaced crescents, the bow of the goddess arranged to form a center panel which encloses a shield bearing three fleurs-de-lis and the initials of Henry and Diane. Certain of the bindings of this king carry a crowned H in each corner and at the sides, while others are entirely covered with intricate designs in painted mosaic with interlacings mingled with the emblems.

The books bound for Henry as Dauphin of France, 1536–1547, are decorated with a semis consisting of a dolphin and fleurs-de-lis, or with a single dolphin in the center ensigned with a crown.

It cannot be told who designed or executed the ornaments for these bindings. The designs are invariably both original and of high merit. The execution in most cases is admirably carried out. During this period the decoration or finishing was the work of the gilder, a distinct class of artisans. The hand of at least three or four different gilders may be traced in the bindings of Henry and Diane.

Realizing the quantity and the superior quality of the works which have been left us from the time of the Renaissance, it must be acknowledged that these gilders worked, not from their own designs, but from sketches made under the supervision of the great artists of the time, who, having made typographic designs as we know, did not hesitate to put their hand to the embellishment of the exteriors of books.

On many of the best bindings executed for Henry II, the entire ornamentation, with the exception of the emblems, was made by means of a series of fillets or segments of circles, which combined to form an infinite variety of arabesques and conventional foliage. It may be because of the paucity of engraved tools employed on these covers that their designs are considered the finest executed in France.

It is very empirical for one to decide just what constitutes a degradation of ornament and design. Herbert P. Horne, in *The Binding of Books,* definitely disagrees with other authorities on these bindings. He says in part, " Fine, no doubt, as this new manner is, it shows less reticence, simplicity, and mastery of effect than are found in the older manner, which preceded it, and from which it is entirely distinct. One cause of this inferiority is to be attributed to an excessive use of curves, and to a consequent neglect of those incomparable decorative effects which are alone to be produced by a proper contrast of curved with angular forms and right lines. . . . Again, not only are too many elements introduced into the designs of these bindings, but, also, these elements are, themselves, not always in due relation to one another."

As an example, Mr. Horne cites a painted binding in which the slight border lines are the only right forms in the whole composition. He also compares a binding for Henry II with one from the collection of Grolier, saying that, although the bindings of both books are ornamented by a fillet intricately interlaced, yet " in the binding executed for the treasurer, the interlacings of this fillet, which is principally

63

worked in right lines, are with great art massed by themselves, and subtly contrasted with the other curved and angular forms of the design. In that executed for the king, the interlacings of this fillet, which is almost entirely worked in curves, form a continuous and intricate border, the principal member of a far less effective design." He further states that the cyphers and devices of the king and his mistress occurring on this binding in varying sizes, figuring together with engraved tools, bear no relation one to another.

His stand, therefore, is that while too many figured tools are employed on these bindings, certain of the effects produced by gouges and fillets would be better and more easily formed by engraved stamps. It would be unfair and unfounded, however, to state that these figured tools made necessary the decadence of ornament, if such it is considered. It is more probable that they proved such an easy way of gaining effect that all restraint in their production was cast aside and therefore they became too complicated.

But, to return to the bindings executed for Henry II, there are now about 800 of his volumes in the Bibliothèque Nationale, which must have made up nearly his whole library. The emblems and designs used on these volumes have produced so much discussion among authorities that they cannot be overlooked in this sketch.

These emblems included his monogram alone and crowned; his monogram with that of his queen,

Catherine de Médicis, the two C's of the queen being interlaced with the H of the king; and his monogram with that of his mistress, Diane de Poitiers, the two D's being interlaced with the H in a manner similar to the monogram of the king and queen; and the crescent, deer, hound, bows, quivers and other emblems of the chase suggested by the name of Diane. The base of the designs is composed of interlacings which are sometimes combined with azured tools. The backs are, for the first time, consistently without bands and the decoration of the back harmonizes with that of the sides.

The crescent moon is said to have been adopted by Henry when he became Dauphin, together with the motto DONEC TOTUM IMPLEAT ORBEM. The cypher of H combined with two D's has already been referred to. It has been suggested that it may mean Henry Deux instead of Henry and Diane, his mistress. Her enemies certainly interpreted it in the latter manner, but its use on certain religious books may seem to stand in the way of this solution. It has also been explained as the cypher of the king and queen, but there is another H interlaced with two C's which is entirely distinct, the C's extending considerably over the sides.

That it is the monogram of Henry and Diane is fairly well assured since this particular cypher is never crowned as is the H alone and the H and C; it being very often accompanied by the symbols of the chase, which Catherine could scarcely claim as her own. In spite of this evidence, it may be well to note some of the claims of the opposition. Léonard Limousin, an artist, pictures Catherine in an enamel wearing a necklace in which this monogram occurs; and in 1575, after the death of both her husband and Diane, the queen caused the crescents and bows and arrows to be introduced into the decorations of the windows of Sainte Chapelle at Vincennes.

It may be supposed that, if these were the symbols of the mistress of her husband, they would be distasteful to her. Furthermore, many of the king's letters to Diane are signed with this monogram. However, a curious illustration of the morals of this time may prove to be the solution of the unusual coincidence.

Certainly, Catherine knew on her arrival in France to marry Henry, Duc d'Orleans, that her position was a difficult one. Her training was such as to make her maintain complete control of her feelings and actions. She, therefore, made every effort to make a friend of Diane instead of exhibiting anger at the expression *seul princesse* which Henry termed his mistress.

Diane, for her part, evinced the greatest deference to the queen and was tireless in her attendance on her health and the welfare of her children. In this way, she was accepted in the royal household as a friend and adviser.

The library of Diane de Poitiers at her Château d'Anet was as celebrated as that of her lover. Even

before her friendship with the Duc d'Orleans, later
Henry II, she gave evidence of her love for books.
In 1531, after the death of her husband, Louis de
Brezé, she adopted a symbol for her bindings consisting of an arrow encircled by laurels rising from
a tomb, and the motto SOLA VIVIT IN ILLO.  Upon
becoming mistress of the Dauphin she deleted the
tomb and changed the motto to SOLA VIVIT IN ILLA,
retaining nothing of a compromising nature, yet
seeming not to abandon the regard for her husband.
M. Bauchart in *Les Femmes Bibliophiles de France*
notes this change and illustrates it with a reproduction of one of her bindings, on the lower board of
which this device appears.  The arms of Brezé impale
those of Poitiers on the upper board.

When Henry succeeded his father, in 1547, he
created Diane de Poitiers Duchess of Valentinois.
Her château at Anet was one of the greatest works
of its kind during the period of the Renaissance.
After the king's death in 1554, Diane retired to Anet,
where she died in 1566.  During these years that
she survived the king, Diane continually added to
her library.

Her remarkable library of vellum manuscripts and
printed books was beautifully bound, and contained
many volumes which were presents from the king.
Her books remained at Anet until 1723, when they
were sold after the death of the Princesse de Condé,
to whom the castle belonged.  M. Bauchart gives a
list of those of her books which he has been able

67

to trace, this list numbering only some thirty-five titles.

Examples of bindings carrying the arms of Henry II and Diane de Poitiers are, as have been suggested, largely limited to the Bibliothèque Nationale. However, single examples are to be found in other great public and private collections. MM. Marius Michel give reproductions of several of the most notable in the French collection in *La Reliure Française*. One of those belonging to Henry is described as a binding which in point of view of the composition and of the execution of the design is one of the most complete of those produced during the Renaissance. This binding covers Herold's *Originum,* printed at Bâle in 1557. It is one of the rare volumes of this monarch which does not carry the emblems. The leather is dark in color with an oval in the center, carrying the arms of France supported by Aldine flowers shaded in the French manner. The arabesques in fillet are on a stippled and lined background. The arms and center plaque are in gold, the remainder of the decoration being silver.

Another example reproduced by this writer is that of Berlinghieri's *Geographia,* which he cites as an outstanding example of the style composed entirely of emblems and interlaced fillets. A wide border encloses in its interstices the crescents and entwining H D monogram. The center panel bears the title of the book and the arms of France, surrounded by the initials, crescents and fleurs-de-lis. A crowned

H appears at each of the four corners outside the fillet.

W. Y. Fletcher describes several bindings from the libraries of these bibliophiles which are now in the British Museum. One of these is in citron morocco, each cover bearing the arms of the king surrounded by the Order of Saint Michel and accompanied by the crescent and his initial. The design is enclosed by bows, tied together with ribbons. An outer border of a corded pattern encloses, besides the center plaque, several emblems — the monogram, fleurs-de-lis and crescents. The book formerly possessed bosses and clasps which have now disappeared. The arms, monogram, fleurs-de-lis and corded border are shown in gold, the bows and crescents alone being painted white.

Another binding in the British Museum is of brown morocco, each cover having an oval inlay of olive morocco carrying the arms of the king, Order of Saint Michel, initials and single crescent inside the joined bows. The arms are in dark gold on the upper cover and in blind on the lower. Initials, crescents, and fleurs-de-lis are worked in with fillet designs which are connected with solid and azured flowers. The back is decorated in harmony with the sides. Clasps and bosses have been lost from this volume. The edges of the leaves are gilt and gauffered.

At least one binding for this king is in the collection of a noted American bibliophile, arriving there from Renouard's collection. It is a magnificent piece in composition and execution with the gilding arranged in compartments in a design of great elegance. The material is green morocco, the entire surface carrying a design composed of flowers and gouges. This example is an exception to the rule of Henry's bindings set forth earlier by Mr. Horne, since the curved lines are beautifully contrasted with oblong- and diamond-shaped fillets, much resembling, in that manner, the bindings executed for Grolier.

At least one example must be cited of the imitation cameo bindings done for Henry II which were mentioned during the discussion of the famous cameo design in the books of Demetrio Canevari. Instead of being made of a lacquered paste put on the leather to hold the shape of the cameo, these imitations are merely stamped on the boards. Mr. Fletcher must again be referred to for a reproduction and description of a binding of this type. The ornament is applied on brown calf; the sides ornamented with a scroll design, decorated in black, white and pink paint, only portions of which still remain. The spaces enclosed by the pattern are studded with gold dots, arranged in groups of three. In the center of each cover is a sunk medallion of Henry II, stamped in gold, his crowned initial being placed on each side of the head.

Catherine de Médicis brought to Henry II a dowry of books which was supplemented with a great love for them, her natural heritage from the Medici

family. This collection comprised some of the manuscripts from the library of Lorenzo de' Medici.

One very considerable portion of her library was
acquired at the death of Marshal Strozzi, who was
killed at the siege of Thionville in 1558. At this
time, Catherine, who was then queen-mother, took
possession of his books. Although she promised to
pay his son, he never received any recompense.

More than 4,000 printed books, in addition to
many manuscripts, are said to have been in her
library at Chenonceaux and in her Château de St.
Maur, near Paris. On her death, in 1588, the library
was saved from her creditors by the activity of her
librarian, Benciveni, Abbé of Bellebranche. De
Thou, in 1594, attempted to have the library revert
to the king, but this was not incorporated in an Act
of Parliament until 1599.

When these books were united with those of the
king, they were mostly rebound with the royal arms
to free them from the dangers of Catherine's creditors. Therefore, we find but a small collection bearing her arms and initials, and many of these are in
private collections.

It cannot be doubted from the examples extant
that the foremost artists decorated these volumes.
All styles of design may be found on these copies,
from the Grolieresque motif through the more intricate style found on the bindings of Henry II, as
well as some done in the so-called Eve style of the
period of Henry III.

71

For the most part, however, they are very richly decorated with a great variety of ornaments. Most frequently they bear the arms of France and an interlaced monogram of the letters H and C. A crowned K often appears on the side or backstrip of the binding. After becoming a widow, the queen often had the *cordelière des veuves* stamped or painted upon the sides, surrounding her arms. Another of her later emblems was a heap of quicklime on which drops of rain were falling, together with the motto, ARDOREM EXTINCTA TESTANTUR VIVERE FLAMMA. The raindrops, signifying tears, show that the heat of love still lives, though there is no flame, since water poured upon lime causes heat without flame.

The decoration on the bindings of Henry II and Diane de Poitiers, as well as the early bindings of Catherine de Médicis which were bound during the reign of this king, were designed by the greatest artists of the time, although it is impossible to record the names of either artists or gilders. Jehan Foucalt and Jehan Louvet were the two most celebrated gilders of the period, but it cannot be definitely said that they exercised their craft upon the ornamentation of bindings. The king himself appears to have occupied some of his leisure hours with this work, for a little chest covered with leather, bearing in the midst of the tooling the motto, REX ME FECIT 1556, is exhibited in the Louvre.

Although the external embellishment of books assumed an exceptional importance during his reign, there were but few private collectors. Margaret d'Angoulême (1492–1549), Queen of Navarre, shared the tastes of her brother, Francis I, and possessed some fine bindings, the general decoration being a series of lozenge-shaped compartments made of reversed curves, separated by marguerites and bearing the crowned monogram of the Duchesse d'Alençon or Queen of Navarre.

Peter Ernest, Comte de Mansfeldt, the celebrated general of Charles V, possessed a fine library, as did also his son, Charles. The constable Anne de Montmorency had many bindings decorated with his sword entwined with a sash.

The death of Henry II brought the great traditions of French binding to a temporary halt, only to raise them to even greater heights during the closing years of the sixteenth century. Of the bindings of Francis II but few are known. The chief decoration of those extant is either a dolphin in gold with plain lines on the side, or, after his coming to the throne, the arms of France with his monogram.

The reign of Francis II, extending from 1559 to 1560, was too short to leave any appreciable influence on art. The most notable of his bindings form part of the work of one of the great gilders of Henry II. An example from the library of this monarch which has found its way to a famous American collection is in brown calf with a small dolphin and fleur-de-lis as the central emblem on each cover. Blind fillet rules form the border, a gold fleur-de-lis appearing at each corner. A fleur-de-lis and bird alternate on the backstrip.

It is left to Charles IX, brother of Francis II, to supply a new manner and a new style in binding. As has been said, four distinct gilders have been found at work on the volumes known to have belonged to Henry II. Now, suddenly, the entire quartet drop from sight and the great bindings of the Renaissance are seen no more.

Apparently, as was the case with many celebrated scientists and artists, they were forced to leave the country as a result of the Huguenot persecutions of 1562 to 1570. It seems probable that these gilders fell victims to this fanaticism, since not only do we find no bindings coming from their hands, but their very tools completely disappear.

The only mode of decoration that survived the Renaissance period is that in which azured corners and centerpieces are used. The execution of these stamps, which is done in press, is such as to allow no judgment other than on the design and engraving of the stamp itself. The manner in which they are engraved, the models, and the way the shading is executed, all tend to prove that these stamps are the ones left by the early sixteenth century workers. They were used throughout the reign of Charles IX and well through the seventeenth century.

The emblem of Charles IX generally has the arms of France in the center, with or without two pillars united by a floating scroll bearing the motto, PIETATE ET JUSTITIA. His bindings are sometimes distinguished by two C's reversed and interwoven generally with K, which, it is supposed, represents the initial of his mother, Catherine de Médicis. The letters are crowned and sometimes are made to form a semis.

It was near the close of the reign of Charles IX that a new style of decoration was introduced. This style is a geometrical interlacing dividing the boards of the cover into compartments of more artistic shapes than had before been made in this manner. These compartments are generally left free from decoration.

When Henry III came to the throne, in 1574, he appropriated this style of decoration. He caused the death head, symbol of the Order of Penitents, to be customarily used on the backs of his books. These backstrips, which were usually without bands, contained at the top the title of the books and at the foot the motto, SPES MEA DEUS. In the central compartment of the recto and verso, he employed plates of the Crucifixion and the Passion.

This was a period of emblems, and seldom were they more misused than by Henry III. He instituted the Order of the Saint Esprit, the symbol of which often appears on his books. His fanaticism led him to use the above mentioned religious seals on all books without regard as to whether they were religious or profane.

Another style of binding adapted by this king has a semis of tears and fleurs-de-lis, or his monogram interlaced with the double lambda of his wife, Louise de Lorraine.

Examples of the bindings from this collection are largely limited to the Bibliothèque Nationale, but the British Museum possesses a fine breviary belonging to Henry III. In the center of the front cover is the Crucifixion and on the back cover the Annunciation. The field is powdered with fleurs-de-lis.

Henry III made certain regulations for the decoration of books, limiting the use of gold in the ornaments. Titles were permitted to be in gold, the edges gilt, and lines and flowers to be traced in gold, but large, solid stamps were forbidden. The effect of this edict was to produce bindings of a charming simplicity.

After the grotesque and irrelevant bindings of the early years of the reign of Henry III, we find new and graceful designs being developed by the French binders. The first of these was an adaptation of an early style, that of the semis or diaper pattern made by repetition of one or more small tools.

With this style, as with the later so-called "fanfare" style, the name of Nicholas Eve is associated. Henry III caused the semis design to be employed, the pattern being formed by tears, fleur-de-lis, or the monogram of the king with two lambdas, representing Louise de Lorraine, his wife. This design is

sometimes used with a representation of the Crucifixion as a centerpiece.

It must be remembered that while Nicholas Eve
held the distinguished title of *Relieur du Roy,* it is
doubtful if he did more than supervise the work of
forwarders and gilders in his shop. The names of
the actual workers on these masterpieces, therefore,
are probably lost forever. Only very few of the
bindings credited to this artist can definitely be
proved to have been done in his shop.

In his *Bookbinding in France,* W. Y. Fletcher reproduced a binding " which is known from reliable
evidence to be Eve's work." This cover bears a
centerpiece of the arms of the king, being combined with the arms of France and Poland, surrounded by the collar of the Order of the Saint
Esprit, and surmounted by a crown bearing the
motto, MANET ULTIMO COELO. A semis of fleurs-de-lis
covers the binding, interrupted by the king's cypher
on all four sides of the arms, and branches of foliage
at the corners.

In 1579, Eve was given the task of binding forty-
two copies of the statutes of the Order of the Saint
Esprit. For this work he received the sum of forty-
seven and a half ecus, or about seven shillings English money of the same period, and probably eighteen to twenty dollars today. These were bound in
an orange morocco, which time has improved by
changing into a rich, warm brown.

The execution of the binding was much the same

as the *Histoires des Faicts des Roys,* already described. The tools, however, are much larger and the semis is composed of a combination of tongues of flames and fleurs-de-lis. Above and below and on each side of the arms is a representation of a dove, the symbol of the Holy Spirit. At each of the four corners is the monogram of Henry and Louise de Lorraine.

The vivacious tastes of Marguerite de Valois, third daughter of Henry II and Catherine de Médicis, and the first wife of Henry IV, did not at all coincide with those of her brother, Henry III. Marguerite inherited a love of books and spent both time and money lavishly on her library.

To meet these tastes, a style was introduced utilizing the geometrical compartment design of Henry III, but adding flowers in each of the ovals. The marguerite was the natural choice of a design and is repeated in various forms. The groundwork was formed of branches of foliage.

This style, coming as it did immediately after the death of the masterpieces of the Renaissance and the complete disappearance of those craftsmen together with their tools, was a happy inspiration of the French gilders, as MM. Marius Michel say. These bindings, which are of the school of Nicholas Eve, created an instantaneous success.

Three distinct manners are to be noted in this general style. In the earliest, such as those already described as belonging to Henry III, the compartments are not filled in at all. The second style, called *à la Fanfare,* is easily distinguished by the presence in the compartments of azured tools of the Lyons school. In the last and most beautiful manner, the interlacings are much more rich, the branches and foliage of the groundwork are more important and the spirals are broken up by azured tailpieces. All details became innumerable and increasingly fine until, in the seventeenth century, the most minute tools were introduced for this decoration.

All amateurs of the period revelled in this kind of gilding and De Thou, the most important collector of the time, had a large number of his bindings treated in this manner. The name of *Fanfare* was given this style when Charles Nodier of the eighteenth century had a volume named *Les Fanfares et Couvrées Abbadesques* bound in this manner by Thouvenin.

The library of Marguerite de Valois contained a great number of choice volumes, nearly all bound in olive, red and citron morocco. The covers, bearing marguerites, are also ornamented with branches of laurel, palm and olive. A beautiful copy in the British Museum of *De Rebus Gestis Francorum* is bound in this style. The geometrical pattern plays an important part, the curves being lined with branches of laurel and palms, with many centerpieces of marguerites.

Another adaptation of this style which is generally credited to Marguerite more likely should be credited to Marie Marguerite de Valois de Saint-Remy, granddaughter of Henry III. Those volumes are tooled with a border of palm and laurel branches enclosing a number of small floral oval compartments, each holding a marguerite or other flower. In the center of the upper cover is a shield charged with three fleurs-de-lis on a bend, a similar shield with three lilies, and the motto, EXPECTA NON ELUDET, appearing on the lower cover. M. Guigard, in his *Armorial du Bibliophile,* points out that these signs and the motto should be attributed to Marie Marguerite. These bindings in all probability came from the workship of Clovis Eve, a brother of Nicholas.

Marie de Médicis, second wife of Henry IV, also had a great love for letters and the arts. Many of her books were bound in the richest taste. The Eve *Fanfare* style is used on some, while others are ornamented with a semis of fleurs-de-lis. Her cypher, either alone or associated with the fleur-de-lis, was sometimes employed. Her arms, being those of France and Tuscany, were often surrounded with the *cordelière,* the sign of her widowhood.

On the less costly of the bindings of the last forty years of the sixteenth century the interlacing strapwork was used only at the center and corners.

Although the date of the death of Nicholas Eve remains unknown, it appears to have occurred during the last decade of the sixteenth century, for in 1596 we find both his brother, Clovis Eve, and George Drobet using the title *Relieur du Roy.* This office was quite commonly held by two persons at the same time during the next century.

Clovis Eve was associated with Pierre Mettayer in the publishing and printing of books, though he, himself, was not a printer. Most of the publishing entered into by this concern was in the field of religious books. They obtained a renewal of privileges to print "*Messels, Breviaries, Diurnaux*," as well as other books concerning the usage of the Council. This was later withdrawn on the objection of Stationers and the University.

The connections proving Clovis Eve to have been a binder appear in the imprint of some few books and in the check rolls of the Royal Household, as well as the books of the Guild of St. Jean. His imprint runs, "*A Paris pour Clovis Eve, Relieur ordinaire du Roy au Mont S. Hylaire.*" His name appears in the books of the king as having received recompense for bindings in the years 1598 to 1633. He was master of the Guild from 1602 to 1604 and the appearance of his name in the books of the Guild shows him to have been a very active member.

Practically no assurance can be obtained that Clovis Eve actually bound any books in the fanfare style which is generally credited to him. From his household accounts, Gaston d'Orleans appears to have paid 33 livres to this binder in 1628 for binding a *Missal* and a *Book of Hours* in Levant morocco with a semis of fleurs-de-lis. M. Léon Gruel in his *Manuel* attributes to Clovis the binding of an *Office de la Semine Saincte* which is tooled in a semis of crowned L's and fleurs-de-lis of Louis XIII. The characters of this semis are large.

As already described, the fanfare bindings attributed to Eve differ totally from this design of ascertained authenticity. Nevertheless, the Eve style continues to bring to mind the geometrical compartments ornamented with branches, foliage and flowers which were so remarkably executed during the tenure of office of the Eves.

Gaston Drobet, also bookseller and binder to Henry IV, moved to Paris from Tours about 1595. M. Gruel reproduces a binding by this artisan which suggests the simplicity of the second decade of the seventeenth century. A double fillet rule appears at the outside edge of the binding, the center of which is ornamented with a single oval composed of branches and foliage. The backstrip is divided into four compartments, each containing a single fleur-de-lis.

Arriving at the end of the sixteenth century, we must note the advances made in bookbinding aside from the province of decoration. Soon after the ascension of Henry II to the throne in 1547, the solidity of the early bindings gave way to a finer treatment. The bands on the backs of the books, which were heavy and numerous, were discarded and a decoration was introduced in harmony with that on the sides. This came into general practice about 1560. In order to avoid these bands, it was necessary to saw across the backs of the books to embed the cord on which the leaves are sewn. During this century, also, the leather began to be pared before covering — a step that advanced greatly the neatness and delicacy of the work.

Guards and end papers of this period are generally of white paper, though vellum or parchment is sometimes used. The use of leather doublures had not yet come into general use. MM. Marius Michel state that the pretended doublures of this period are only stamped covers taken from other books and applied more or less carefully on the inside cover. The edges of hooks were often ornamented with designs similar to those employed on the sides. They were carried out by means of matting tools. A marker of silk or ribbon was also added to most books of this period. These markers were often ornamented with precious stones.

Henry IV devoted very little time to any other art than that of architecture during his twenty-one years of sovereignty. Due to the religious disturbances of the period, bookbinding as well as other forms of decoration suffered a decline in taste and execution. A binding for this monarch which is in the Bibliothèque Nationale illustrates this point.

M. Gruel describes the ensemble of this binding as rich, but criticizes the lack of character, invention and originality in its conception and the lack of strength in its execution. It is in red Levant morocco; the border is composed of a semis of fleurs-de-lis, interrupted at intervals by the insertion of oval plaques in mosaic, containing the initial H or the the cypher H D B crowned. This semis is bordered on each side by a fillet rule and a running design. Each corner is ornamented by palm and olive branches as well as the crowned cypher and semis of fleurs-de-lis. The center is in the shape of a diamond composed of the same ornaments surrounding the arms of the king.

During this period, Jacques Auguste de Thou was the outstanding figure as a patron of bookbinding. He was born at Paris in 1553, the son of Christophe de Thou, himself a very famous collector. Jacques Auguste inherited the library of his father, which contained several books presented to him by Grolier as tokens of gratitude to him for having saved his life and honor at a very critical time in his official career. Jacques Auguste had previously inherited the library of his uncle, Adrian de Thou, which gave him an excellent basis on which to develop a library of magnitude through the purchase of libraries and single volumes. His collection finally totalled more than one thousand manuscripts and eight thousand printed books.

The arms of De Thou varied considerably as a result of his two marriages. His own arms were argent, a chevron between gadflies sable. His name appeared on a scroll below the escutcheon, the whole enclosed between two branches of laurel. His monogram, I.A.D.T., later replaced his name. After his

marriage to Marie Barbançon, he impaled his wife's
arms with his own and changed his monogram to
I.A.M. (Jacques Auguste, Marie). After the death
of Marie in 1601, he married Gasparde de la Chastre,
placing her arms in the position of those of his former
wife and changing the monogram to I.A.G. The
arrangement of each of these monograms is said by
some authorities to be such as to form a Greek
theta to represent Thou.

De Thou died on May 7, 1617. His library has
the distinction of having remained in the family for
several generations before it was finally sold. His
eldest son, François Auguste, retained the collection
until September 12, 1642, when he was beheaded at
Lyons for alleged participation in the conspiracy of
Cinq-Mars.

The third son, Jacques Auguste, then acquired the
library, which he enriched by adding to it the collection of his father-in-law, Hugues Picardet. He
died in 1677, leaving his treasures to the Abbé de
Sameraux-Bois, also named Jacques Auguste de
Thou, who sold them three years later to meet the
creditors of the family. Cherron de Menars bought
it intact except for certain manuscripts which went
to the library of the king. In 1706 it was sold to the
Bishop of Strasburg, who left it to his nephew, the
Prince de Soubise, by whom it was finally dispersed
in 1788.

Because of the popularity of fanfare bindings during this period, it is generally supposed that de Thou

had a large portion of his library bound in this manner. It is true that he caused many excellent examples of this style to be made for him, but by far
the larger part of his collection was plainly bound in
rich red morocco with his arms — a style that later
was much copied in every country.

Although many of the bindings done for Henry
IV were heavily decorated with gold tooling, some
few examples are extant in which a more simple style
was followed. Of this class is the binding of an
*Arrests sur Quelques Questions Notables* in a great
American collection. This cover is in a brown morocco with all tooling in blind. The arms of the
king are impressed in the center of the sides and a
crowned fleur-de-lis is at each of the corners inside
a triple fillet rule. The backstrip is decorated with
three large crowned fleurs-de-lis equidistant from
each other, and the intervening spaces are filled with
small fleurs-de-lis.

A binding of a somewhat similar style which appears to have come from the library of this sovereign
is in the British Museum. It covers Part I of de
Thou's *Historiarum sui Temporis* and is supposed
to have been presented to James I, King of England,
by the author. Since it was presented with the per-
mission of Henry IV, it may have come from his own
library or it may have been specially bound for
James. It is in red morocco, bearing on each cover,
within a filleted panel with crowned fleurs-de-lis at
the angles, the arms of Henry IV, ensigned with the

royal crown and surrounded by the Orders of Saint
Michel and the Saint Esprit. A large crowned
fleur-de-lis is above and below the arms, a smaller
one appearing at the sides. The space between the
border and the panel is decorated with two large
and two small crowned H's, the large ones carrying
the numeral IIII. The back is decorated with alternate crowned H's and crowned fleurs-de-lis.

Marie de Médicis, the wife of Henry IV, continued
and greatly enlarged her library after the death of
the king. Her bindings are found with the arms of
France and Tuscany. The remainder of the cover is
stamped in a semis of fleurs-de-lis except the corners,
which carry the queen's crowned cypher.

Under the reign of Louis XIII, the art of bookbinding again revived, although little of great importance was produced. The principal form of decoration was the semis of initials or cyphers, but an
increasing number of artistic people devoted a part
of their time to the study and collection of bindings
of beauty.

Among these private collectors were La Vieuville,
Philippe du Plessis-Mornay, Michel Le Tellier, le
Comte de Mansfeld and Cardinal de Richelieu. At
this time all the Beaux-Arts displayed a reawakening.

A binding for Louis XIII reproduced by M. Gruel
is done in an olive-green morocco decorated throughout by a semis composed of a double lambda crowned,
the cypher of the king. In the center occur the
arms of France and Navarre.

An American collection contains a binding in red morocco for Louis XIII, carrying his arms in the center surmounted with the royal crown. A semis of the letter L crowned and the fleur-de-lis covers sides and back. A double border is formed of a lace pattern.

Before becoming king, the books of Louis XIII generally bear his arms as Dauphin of France, the covers being figured with a semis of dolphins and fleurs-de-lis and a double lambda occurring at the four corners. After his ascension to the throne, he used the fleur-de-lis, crowned initial, and crowned double lambda in a diaper pattern.

A binding for Anne of Austria, queen of Louis XIII, is in olive morocco with the sides ornamented with a semis of fleurs-de-lis and a central stamp of the arms of France and Austria. The border of this binding is composed of two double fillets, and two dotted rules divided by a running design.

Some bindings for Louis XIII and Anne of Austria are decorated with a delicate lace tooling. These bear the crowned initial of the king and the crowned cypher of Queen Anne, being two A's, one of them inverted. This style is attributed to Macé Ruette, who succeeded Clovis Eve.

Macé Ruette is supposed to have introduced into France marbled paper and also a yellow marbled morocco. The origin of marbled paper is most obscure. It has been credited to Holland, Germany and Turkey. La Caille in 1689 assigned its origin to

Ruette. John Kunckel, in 1679, ascribes it to Germany and describes its manufacture. Lord Bacon describes it as a Turkish invention, saying:

"The Turks have a pretty art of chamoletting of paper, which is not with us in use. They take divers oyled colours and put them severally (in drops) upon water; and stirre the water lightly, and then wet their paper (being of some thicknesse) with it, and the paper will be waved, and veined, like chamolet or marble."

In 1889, the South Kensington Art Library purchased an album containing 228 leaves, of which forty-six are of marbled paper, comprising no fewer than thirty-four varieties. This book, according to our authority, Sarah T. Prideaux, belonged to Wolffgang, of Vienna, who left there in 1616 for Constantinople, where he stayed for eight years. The dates of entry appearing in this album extend from 1616 to 1632.

From these facts, Miss Prideaux arrives at the conclusion that "marbled paper in its varieties was therefore most probably of Turkish invention, as the hitherto known examples, French or Dutch, which can be attributed to a date prior to 1680, are all on one class, the small comb variety."

With the second quarter of the seventeenth century, a new figure appears in bookbinding history; that of the mysterious Le Gascon. Until very recently, it has been doubted that there really was such a person and his works have often been credited to other known binders of the period, chief of these being Florimond Badier. M. Thoinan in *Les Relieurs Français* has definitely indicated that Le Gascon was not a mythical character by discovering several documents referring to him.

The earliest of these documents appears on the register of the Guild of St. Jean in the year 1622, being an entry of payments made to him for materials used in binding a missal for the use of the Guild. Since no charge for labor is included, it may be assumed that Le Gascon contributed his services. The volume is described as *doré à petits fers* on red morocco. Peiresc and Dupuy, noted collectors of the day, refer to Le Gascon in letters, Peiresc having complained to Dupuy that Le Gascon had badly cropped a book. Dupuy, in turn, expresses surprise, saying that Le Gascon is *assez scrupuleux*.

Again Dupuy refers to Le Gascon as the binder of a copy of the works of *Tertullian* which Peiresc intended selling to an Italian cardinal. François Auguste de Thou in a letter to Dupuy also mentions this binder in connection with a copy of the Koran he secured in Alexandria, saying, "*la reliure vous plaira, et je m'assure que Le Gascon s'étudiera d'imiter dorure.*"

These notes, while proving the existence of such a person, and showing him to be both binder and gilder, do not definitely identify him. M. Gruel, in his *Manuel Historique et Bibliographique de l'Amateur de Reliure,* seems to incline slightly to the belief that Badier is the real Le Gascon, although he admits his inability to understand why Badier should sign some of his less attractive work and leave certain masterpieces without a signature. Moreover, the records of the Guild show that Le Gascon was already a craftsman of some experience in 1622, while Badier is said to have been apprenticed to Jean Thomas, a gilder, in 1630 and to have become a master binder only in 1645.

The sign of the " couped head," a head in dotted outline and cut off close at the neck, is but little help in solving the Le Gascon problem. This sign, which has come to be considered the mark, even perhaps the likeness, of the unknown master, appears on many of the bindings supposedly done by him.

Only two books are known to be in existence which are traditionally said to have been bound by Le Gascon. These are the *Guirlande de Julie* and a volume of *Prayers* by Madame de Rambouillet. They are both bound in red morocco with a semis of the letters I and L in the first case and V in the Prayers. Each of these books contain a doublure, the former being decorated with a semis and the latter in the style of the double fillet.

These definitely known bindings of Le Gascon differ greatly from those generally ascribed to him, such as that reproduced by M. Gruel, which is done in geometrical compartments with *pointille* or dotted ornaments filling many of the important interstices. The couped head in dotted outline appears at each of the four corners and the border outside a double fillet is of a *dentelle* nature.

W. Y. Fletcher reproduces several examples of so-called Le Gascon work. One is described as bound in red morocco, the sides and back being exquisitely adorned with very delicate tooling, partly solid and partly *au pointille*. Another is a binding for the Bishop of Meaux in red morocco, the sides and back being decorated with beautiful fine tooling, principally *au pointille,* enclosed in geometrical patterns. The arms and cypher of the Bishop appear on the sides. Both of these bindings carry the typical Le Gascon *dentelle* border.

Although it is strange that these bindings, differing as they do from his known work, should be credited to Le Gascon, it is even more difficult to ascribe them to Badier, since the signed work of Badier in this style of decoration is far inferior to the so-called Le Gascon bindings. The Bibliothèque Nationale has a copy of the *De Imitatione Christi,* 1640, richly bound in this very manner and signed FLORIMOND BADIER FECIT. INV. MM. Marius Michel claim this to be the work of an inferior imitator. M. Gruel, however, insists on the importance of Badier's work.

In mentioning the *Imitatione* of Badier, W. H. J. Weale says, ". . . he [Badier] proudly signed at the foot of the lining: FLORIMOND BADIER FECIT. INV. . . . He was an inferior workman who managed to copy the real man's work on the outside, but made a dead

failure of the decoration of the lining." MM. Marius
Michel say of this binding, " *Fecit,* malheureuse-
ment; *invenit,* jamais! "

Florimond Badier is thought to have come to Paris
from Gascony, being apprenticed in 1630 and becoming a free member of the Guild of St. Jean in
1645, during which same year he married the daughter of Jean Gillede, a binder. The copy of the *Imitatione* referred to as bearing the signature of Badier
is bound in red morocco, inlaid with colored leathers.
These colored leathers are in compartments formed
by interlaced fillets. The doublure is of citron morocco inlaid in a slightly different manner than that
followed on the exterior. The entire figured work
is *au pointille.*

M. Thoinan believes this to have been an early
example of Badier's work and, as such, he thinks it
most creditable. This binding, in addition to Badier's signature, carries the couped head which has
passed as the mark of Le Gascon. M. Thoinan,
however, believes it may well be the mark of Badier,
thereby arguing that all the bindings on which it is
used were by him. This is based on the belief that
the tools used in these bindings are identical with
those on the signed binding of the *Imitation.*

This theory is strengthened since, although Le
Gascon was a binder of merit in 1622, the style attributed to him did not come into use until 1640 to
1665. However, it may be that Le Gascon was employed in the shop of the Eves and that his adapta-

tion of the geometrical pattern of the Eves in conjunction with his own *pointille* decoration was a tardy development. M. Thoinan closes his inquiry into the history of Le Gascon with the very plausible suggestion that Le Gascon was none other than Jean Gillede, whose daughter Badier married and to whose trade he succeeded.

A binding in mosaic attributed to Le Gascon is reproduced by Fletcher, who terms it a magnificent binding of the first half of the seventeenth century, executed by Le Gascon. The leather is red morocco, the sides and back being inlaid with compartments of light and dark olive, citron, and brown morocco. The whole is elaborately decorated with very delicate tooling, largely *au pointille*.

The genuine work of Le Gascon is nearly always done on red morocco of a peculiar tint which he seems to have introduced as a binding material. His decorations invariably include the outline of interlacing bands enclosing geometrical compartments as the groundwork of all his more decorative work. The red interlacing bands which remain without tooling show out vigorously on the ground of *pointille* tooling.

Le Gascon had a host of imitators, none of whom could surpass him. Some, doubtless, were his pupils, as he, himself, had probably been a pupil of the Eves. Others merely imitated his work with reproductions of his tools.

Le Gascon bound for Habert de Montmort several

94

little volumes decorated with straight and curved
fillets with vases of flowers and *pointille* ornaments
at the corners.

Antoine Ruette, son of Macé Ruette, was born in
1609 and succeeded to the title of Binder in Ordinary
to Louis XIV on the death of his father. His first
signature bearing this title appears in a book which
he published in 1644. The appointment was con-
firmed in 1650 when he received a grant of lodging
for life in the Collège Royal and a salary as Binder
in Ordinary to the king of a hundred livres a year.

A binding executed by him for Anne of Austria
is reproduced by M. Gruel. It carries the arms of
the Queen regent, surrounded by her widow's cords,
her cypher of the double A with one inverted and the
royal crown. He also bound for the Chancellor
Séguier, as well as for Louis XIV. A copy bound
for the king is in the British Museum, the arms of
Louis having been stamped over with the cypher of
George III of England.

This binding is of green morocco with a doublure
of red morocco. *Pointille* tooling plays a large part
in the exterior decoration, but the inside decorations
are in solid line.

The private collectors of this period include the
Chancellor Séguier, whose motto, ARTE ET MARTE, appears on all his bindings together with the golden
fleece. Mornay, Philippede, Richelieu and La Vril-
lière also appear in this period. Pierre and Jacques
Dupuy, of whom some mention has already been

made, were also among the great collectors of the time.

Throughout the reign of Louis XIV, the list of private collectors increased and the number of bindings increased in proportion. Florimond Badier as well as Antoine Ruette bound for the king. To Badier is given credit for the first important use of doublures, though their introduction occurred some years earlier. The first known doublure appears on an Italian binding of 1550 which is now in the Bibliothèque Nationale, but their return is very rare until the time of Louis XIV.

Antoine Ruette was succeeded as royal binder by Claude Le Mire, who held the office together with Gilles Dubois. On the death of Le Mire in 1698, Antoine Boyet received the appointment and held it for a period of thirty-five years. This binder ornamented books in a more severe manner than had been employed previously. His bindings are plainly tooled, the decoration consisting only of a rectangular fillet of gold lines, sometimes with a slight decoration at the angles, and with a coat-of-arms in the center. The forwarding of his books, however, denotes great strength and his bindings are often executed with excellent doublures.

Boyet also may have bound many of the books in the so-called Jansenist style. These bindings are named after the ascetic sect and are characterized by their austerity of style, although their doublures are frequently richly tooled. The amateurs for whom

Boyet worked indicate a constantly increasing list
of persons interested both in literature and bookmaking. He is said to have worked for Colbert,
Flechier, Bishop of Nismes, Longpierre and Count
von Hoym, as well as other collectors.

Colbert managed the affairs of Cardinal Mazarin,
who placed him in a position to receive confidences
from Louis XIV. Colbert was made Minister and
Secretary of State and Controller-General of the
Finances of France. He restored the shattered
finances of the State and increased the royal library
from 16,000 to 40,000 volumes. His own library
contained about 8,000 rare manuscripts and 50,000
printed books, nearly all of which were richly bound
in a beautiful morocco which he obtained specially
through an article in a treaty with the Sultan. Colbert's arms appear on the sides of these books, while
his initials, interlaced and surmounted by a coronet,
occupy the panels of the back. His grandson dis-
posed of the printed books by auction and sold many
of the manuscripts. Most of these volumes were
later secured by Louis XV for the royal library.

Hilaire Bernard de Requeleyne, Baron of Longe-
pierre, used as his book decoration the Golden Fleece
in honor of the success created by his drama *Médée*.
This ornament of the Golden Fleece is the sole decoration of these books, and it generally appears impressed in the center and at the corners of both
boards and in the panels of the back.

A recent bookseller's catalogue carries an illustra-

97

tion of a binding probably executed by Boyet, carrying a triple gold fillet border and the arms of Count von Hoym on the cover. This binding is one of a two-volume set, both of which are listed at $300. The description says that " on Hoym's death they passed into the hands of John Baptiste Colbert, and contain the inscription, BIBLIOTHECAE COLBERTINAE, on each title page. . . . Morocco bindings, with the arms of Count von Hoym, are among the most treasured books bound at this period. Hoym employed three famous binders of his time: Boyet, Du Seuil, and Padeloup. It is usually presumed that Boyet did most of the work, and is very probable that the two present volumes were bound by him."

Augustin Du Seuil has left no authenticated example of his binding, but he is known to have been a craftsman of great repute and to have bound for the great amateurs of the time. He was appointed binder in ordinary to Louis XV in 1717 at the suggestion of the Duchesse de Berry. M. Gruel can find no definite reference to this binder other than his appointment as Binder in Ordinary to the king. The style generally attributed to him is somewhat similar to that employed earlier by Boyet and other binders of less note.

Antoine Michel Padeloup, known as Padeloup le jeune, was the most celebrated of a great family of bookbinders and stationers. The earliest of the family on record is Antoine Padeloup, who was apprenticed to Nicolas Guerard in 1622, obtaining his warrant as master binder ten years later. François Padeloup, the last binder of the family, was still working late in the eighteenth century. Antoine Michel Padeloup was of the third generation of the family in the craft. He was born December 22, 1685. Michel Padeloup, his father, served as his master in teaching him the art of bookbinding.

The appointment of *Relieur du Roy* came to Padeloup le jeune on the death of Luc Antoine Boyet. His bindings, which were executed for the chief collectors of the time, including Count von Hoym and Madame de Pompadour, are famed for the beauty of the leather and the solidity of the forwarding, as well as the grace and effectiveness of the tooling which ornaments the more important volumes. His practice of inserting a ticket in each book he bound is a great aid in determining the work of this craftsman. In some cases, however, there is some doubt that the ticket may have been overlooked or that it may have been removed.

Some of the designs used by Padeloup in his bindings were simple, while others were very elaborate, being done in a mosaic style. His bindings were generally very well executed, the ornaments being combined with the skill of an artist. He worked for Madame de Pompadour, Bonnier de la Mosson and other celebrated collectors of the time.

The tickets which he inserted in his books usually read " *Relié par Padeloup le jeune, Place Sorbonne à Paris.*" In 1733 he bound a volume, inserting a card which reads " *Relieur ordinaire du Roy de Portugal.*" This office he appears to have vacated in 1744 in favor of his son Jean.

One of the principal styles of decoration used by Padeloup le jeune consists of lace borders which are of great beauty and richness. Many of his bindings are further embellished with doublures. Gruel reproduces a binding of this style in which the *dentelle* border forms a cartouche at each of the corners to receive the arms of the collector, while the arms of France are impressed in the center of the cover. A binding reproduced by Fletcher shows the mosaic style which is done in the form of a semis. This volume is covered in brown morocco, inlaid with olive and red morocco and gold tooled. The insides of the covers are lined with red morocco tooled with a beautiful gold border which encloses the arms of the Duchess of Orleans.

Another Padeloup binding, this time for the Duke of Orleans, Regent of France, is in red, blue and citron morocco, elaborately tooled in gold and carrying on each cover the arms of the duke. Several mosaic bindings in the Padeloup style are reproduced by MM. Marius Michel who explain that their best quality consists in the happy choice of colors he makes.

Padeloup le jeune was succeeded by Louis Douceur as binder to the king. This binder worked in the same style as did Padeloup, but his bindings were heavier and more clumsy. Padeloup was the first to use large engraved plates for gold work. These plates were used in an arming press.

Jean Charles Henri Lemonnier, binder to the Duke of Orleans in 1757, was also one of a large family of binders. His mosaics, representing landscapes, allegorical scenes and flowers, are more striking than decorative.

The binders bearing the name of Derome are even more numerous than those of the Padeloup family. Thoinan lists no less than eighteen Deromes in the binding craft as against fifteen Padeloups. Jacques Antoine Derome was the contemporary of Padeloup and is known to have done some excellent work, but his reputation is obscured by the greater brilliancy of his son, Nicolas Denis Derome, who is generally referred to simply as Derome.

The designs of this binder strongly resemble some of those executed by Padeloup and rival them in beauty and in strength of finishing.

It has been suggested with good foundation that Derome secured the materials and stamps of Padeloup, whose wife carried on his business of binding for some years. If this contention is true, it explains the great similarity in the work of these two artists. Derome executed many bindings in mosaic, but his chief fame rests in the *dentelle* borders which he designed and in which he introduced a small bird with wings outstretched and which are known as *dentelle à l'oiseau*.

Derome seems to have adapted designs of the other

crafts to the requirements of bookbindings, and many of these *dentelle* borders may be based on the art of ironwork of the eighteenth century. His designs, being made of tools in combination rather than in repetition, show a greater variety than those of Padeloup. This binder also distinguished his work by use of *etiquettes* of tickets.

Fletcher reproduces a Derome binding in red morocco, the sides of which are ornamented with an elaborate and graceful border. The insides of the covers and the endpapers are lined with blue watered silk. He also reproduces a work of Lemonnier in red morocco, ornamented with flowers formed by inlaid leathers of various colors. The flowers are principally cream-colored and the leaves are olive; the outlines and fibres being executed in gold tooling. The name of the binder is twice stamped on each cover.

The bindings of Louis XV are in the main decorated in the simpler manner of a border of fillet lines with his arms in the center. Each of his daughters also formed a choice collection of books. The books of Madame Adelaide were in red morocco; those of Madame Sophie in citron morocco; and of Madame Victoire in olive morocco. Their arms are always impressed on the covers. At the time of the Revolution, these books were all confiscated and most of them set up in the library of Versailles.

Jeanne Antoinette Poisson, Marquise de Pompadour, collected a library of upwards of 3,000 books,

many of which were well though plainly bound.
These bindings always carry the arms of Madame
de Pompadour in the center of the cover, and generally are further decorated with a floral or plain
line border. Padeloup, Derome and Louis Douceur
are all represented in her bindings.

Madame du Barry, who scarcely read or wrote,
considered a library to be a necessity for every
woman of fashion. Bisiaux generally bound her
books, using red morocco, with her arms and motto
upon the sides.

The books of Louis XVI were also bound in red
morocco and with the minimum of decoration. Before becoming king, his books are decorated with the
arms of the dauphin, this shield later giving way to
the arms of the King of France. His queen, Marie
Antoinette, had a great liking for books, forming
libraries both at the Tuileries and at the Petit
Trianon. The collection at the Tuileries, which was
made up of nearly 5,000 volumes, was confiscated by
a decree of the Convention, and was placed in the
Bibliothèque Nationale in 1793. Some few copies,
however, escaped and have found their way to
private libraries.

Her library at the Petit Trianon was composed
largely of novels and tales of romance, whereas the
larger collection comprised the great literature of
France, Italy and England. The books in English
bore English bindings. The earlier bindings of this
queen far surpass those of her later years. The bind-

ings in the library at the Tuileries are generally made of red morocco with her arms on the sides. These are said to have been executed by a binder named Blaizot. The bindings in the Trianon library are either in half or full calf and, in addition to the arms, bear the initials C. T. (Château de Trianon) surmounted by a crown.

Pierre Paul Dubuisson succeeded Michel Antoine Padeloup as Binder in Ordinary to the King. Dubuisson appears to have been a gilder rather than binder, since some of his books have a label reading *"Doré par Dubuisson, rue St. Jacques."* This gilder made a great study of heraldry, making a very remarkable collection of books relating to this subject. He published a work in two volumes on heraldry in the year 1757. This work he did in conjunction with Gastelier de La Tour.

Dubuisson died in 1762, being succeeded by Pierre Antoine Laferte, who is regarded as one of the best craftsmen of his day. Other members of the Laferte family were also good binders of this period, as were Pierre Vente and Jean Pierre Jubert. The family of Anguerrand also supplied several binders, the best of whom was Pierre Anguerrand, who bound for the Marquis de Paulmy between the years 1770 and 1775. *Dentelle* borders, many of which were excessively massive, were the order of the day.

At the close of the eighteenth century, bookbinding in France began to decline. The very increase in the number of books, of course, played a large part in this decline, which was evident in all branches, including forwarding as well as the design and execution of the gilding.

With the French Revolution, every form of fine art including bindings came to an abrupt end. The troubles and excesses of this period cut short the careers of the great collectors and their libraries were confiscated by the Convention. The few bindings that do appear during this time of stress carry only patriotic emblems, such as the Phrygian bonnet, a figure of Liberty or a sheaf of spears. The Carnavalet Museum has an interesting collection of the tools used on these books.

The establishment of the Empire in 1804 brought about a slow revival of the interest in the arts. Aside from Bozerian, whose works have not succeeded in living, Thouvenin first restored the art of binding to its former place in France. Courteval, Lefevre and Simier were also of this period.

Purgold made a definite effort at this time to reform the methods of forwarding, and it is from his workshop that Bauzonnet proceeded and, with Trautz, came to be among the noted binders of the nineteenth century. Trautz served his apprenticeship in Heidelberg, and in 1833 became associated with Bauzonnet, his future father-in-law. The bindings of Trautz are excellent as regards forwarding as well as decoration. Moreover, he succeeded in securing a better grade of leather than had been obtainable since the Revolution. The single objection to his work is that the backs are rounded to excess, making the books open with difficulty.

Cuzin, Lortic, Niedrée, Duru and Capé must also be mentioned. The great error of this entire period, however, is that it shows not the slightest tendency to originality, but goes on copying the old designs slavishly.

With the end of the nineteenth century came the first signs of digression from the old manner. Léon Gruel, Marius Michel and his son Henri Marius Michel have played a great part in the advance of bookbinding in France, not only by their examples, but by their writings as well. This modern movement in bookbinding may be said to have arisen about 1860, and was further strengthened in 1874 by the organization of about fifty collectors who called themselves "*Les Amis des Livres.*" From this association appeared many books in small editions on paper of high quality which were suited to the expenditure of more effort in the binding operations.

New clubs were formed fast upon the heels of the first one. Soon there came into being several groups whose desire it was to gather together in suitable habit the best books of the day in much the same manner as Grolier took the best books of his day for ornamentation rather than going back to the manuscripts of the earlier scribes.

Research for new motives of decoration led Marius Michel further on the road that he had already taken as an apprentice to Léon Gruel. In 1866, Henri

Marius Michel, undertook to carry on the traditions of his father. In this position, he had great difficulty in overcoming the so-called Trautz mania. Every collector of this period clamored for Trautz bindings until the market was so laden with the works of this craftsman that an inevitable reaction in favor of the more original work of the younger Michel finally took place.

Henri Marius Michel soon was forced to give up the actual work of gilding, devoting his entire attention to the development of new ideas. He did, however, continue to execute the *cuir ciselé*, in which style he is scarcely surpassed. Another style that has become associated with his name is that in which slightly conventionalized flower motives are employed.

This release from the former styles of design naturally brought about a flood of eccentric work which is often characterized by a complete lack of conception and technique.

Léon Gruel, as head of a large workshop, kept much more closely to the accustomed standards than did Michel and great discussions took place between these two authorities as to the proper method of procedure. Certainly a new motive of book decoration is not to be worked out in a short space of time nor was this Michel's intention. Many collectors as well as binders and gilders do feel that a new style must inevitably be worked out that will be more suitable to the style and content of the modern book.

While such a style would be desirable, it must be arrived at in a natural way. Since it is true that we can not escape the spirit of the times in which we live, it is not to be doubted that a sympathetic style will be developed.

## Chapter IV

## BINDING IN ENGLAND

THE ENGLISH BLIND STAMPED leather bindings of the twelfth century have already been described, as have also the bindings in velvet and those in which embroidery was employed as ornament. It was the English stamped bindings, however, for which this country was particularly noted. W. H. James Weale has made a careful examination of all bindings in this style and has presented us with a detailed study of their ornamentation.

With the exception of a very few scattering volumes the study of early English volumes must be carried on through a study of the monasteries rather than through any royal collection. With the introduction of the art of gold tooling, however, the study may be resumed through the medium of the reigning sovereigns who furthered the art in much the same manner as did the French kings. Twice in English history has the existing royal collection been presented to the nation.

The Old Royal Library, which contains manuscripts from the reign of Richard III, was enlarged by each succeeding ruler, until the time of Prince Henry, the oldest son of James I. Prince Henry added greatly to the collection by the expenditure of a large amount of his personal income. On his death, it became the property of James I and, in 1757, it was presented by George II to the nation. There were at this time about 15,000 volumes in the collection.

George III, through agents who were carefully selected, set to work to form a new collection. The greater part of this collection was in modern bindings, although some considerable number remain in their original bindings. In these cases, however, the king caused his arms to be placed in a prominent place on the binding, thereby disfiguring them to a great degree. This collection, comprising some 65,-000 volumes, was presented to the nation by George IV in 1823 and may now be found in the King's Library in the British Museum.

Before printing was introduced into England in the fifteenth century by William Caxton, there seems to have been no attempt on the part of any English sovereign to make any special collection of books. It may be, however, that any collection thus made may have been destroyed by the early Tudor kings in order to retrieve the gems and precious metals which ordinarily decorated the mediaeval bindings. On the other hand, it may be argued that Henry VIII and Edward VI would scarcely have destroyed any bindings which already formed part of a royal collection. Nevertheless, it is true that if there ever was such an early collection of books or bindings in England, all trace of it is now lost.

The art of gold tooling was introduced in England soon after the appearance of the printing press. To Thomas Berthelet must be accredited the honor of being the first English binder to employ this new medium of decoration. Berthelet was the second after Richard Pynson who had the distinction of being made king's printer, his patent being dated February 22, 1530. Many of the bindings from his workshop, gilded on white leather, sometimes deer-skin, sometimes vellum, are very delightful. A binding in this style covers an *Image of Governance* by Sir Thomas Elyot and printed by Berthelet in 1541. This binding carries the same design on each side. A panel enclosed by an ornamental fillet contains an arrangement of curves forming a central plate carrying the words DIEU ET MON DROIT; and at each side of this are the royal initials. At each of the inner corners is a large set stamp, and the ground is dotted over with small circles and a daisy, — a badge used by the Tudors. On the edges are painted in gold the words REX IN AETERNUM VIVE.

The designs employed by Berthelet are admittedly copied from the existing styles on the continent. His bills which have been preserved often describe a book as being " *bounde after the Italian fascion* " or " *after the fascion of Venice.*"

Books bound for Edward VI are more numerous than those done for Henry VIII. Berthelet appears to have bound for this king both before and after his ascension to the throne. One book bound for this king is the first instance of an English book carrying a decorative doublure. The book, a small duodecimo, is covered in crimson velvet and is a collection of *certeine prayers and godly meditacyons,* printed at Malborow in 1538. The inner side of each of the boards is covered with calf, the design being outlined in gold and filled in with colors. These colors lie evenly on the surface of the leather and present a polished surface. This doublure is in a remarkable state of preservation.

The chief English private collectors of this period were Thomas Wotton, 1521–1587, called the English Grolier; Archbishop Cranmer; Lord Treasurer Burghley and Robert Dudley, Earl of Leicester. Stamps of considerable merit occur on the bindings produced for Archbishop Parker, also of this period. The collector Wotton adapted for his use the legend of Grolier, revising it to read THOMAS WOTTONI ET AMICORUM. His arms alone also occur at times. The designs on his books were conceived in the same manner as were those of Grolier. His books are generally bound in calf, with tooled interlacings outlined in gold and painted black.

Robert Dudley, Earl of Leicester, who was Queen Elizabeth's favorite, had a large collection of finely bound books. These are generally very simple, having no ornament other than his device, a bear and ragged staff stamped in the center of each side, together with his initials and a plain line rule.

The bindings of Henry VIII were for the most

part done either in stamped leather or in beautifully embroidered velvets. William Y. Fletcher in *English Bookbindings* illustrates several bindings from the library of this king. Among these reproductions is the binding of the *Image of Governance,* already described. Another example of gold tooling shown is that of a *Commentary on the Campaign of the Emperor Charles V against the French in 1554.* This is among the most elaborate bindings done by Berthelet for Henry VIII. It is in brown leather, having on each cover a vertical panel with the arms of the king, ensigned with the royal crown and carrying the initials H.R. An oblong tablet with inscriptions appears above and below the arms. On each side of the center panels are two circular medallions containing the heads of Plato and Dido. Aldine and Italian borders and ornaments appear on both covers.

A binding for Edward, Prince of Wales, is also here shown. It is in light brown calf, each cover having a centerpiece of a circle of rays and flames, within which appear his badge, motto and initials. Graceful arabesque tooling surrounds the circle and the whole is enclosed in a border of Italian character. After his ascension to the throne, Edward VI continued to give his patronage to Berthelet, as is seen in the binding of a *Historiae Venetae* which was evidently done either by or under the superintendence of this master. The sides of this beautiful binding in brown calf are decorated with a geometrical and arabesque design in black and gold. The central compartment formed by this design carries the arms of the king and smaller compartments at the sides carry his initials, which are crowned. Compartments at the top and bottom contain his motto and the date. The back of this book is interesting in that it is finished in imitation of a fore-edge, being concave and ornamented in gilt and gauffered.

The great majority of the panel-stamped bindings of this period appear to have been for trade editions, although they do, at times, carry the royal arms. Certain books are known to carry arms of Queen Katharine of Aragon, ensigned with the royal crown and supported by two angels. This same design is also employed with the substitution of the arms of Queen Anne Boleyn in place of those of Queen Katharine. There is, however, no known instance of the use of these stamps on any royal book. The book which Anne Boleyn carried with her to the scaffold, a copy of the New Testament in vellum, has, unfortunately, been rebound. This queen made a strange request in regard to her execution. Having but little faith in the clumsy ax which was customarily used for this purpose, she petitioned that she might be executed with a sword after the French fashion. Since no executioner could be found in England who was adept at the use of the sword, it was necessary to secure one from the Continent. In spite of the long delay caused by this unexpected event, it was found after the execution that no coffin had been provided.

Another queen who met her death in a like manner was Lady Jane Grey, a cousin of the boy king, Edward VI. Lady Jane Grey came to this end through no fault of her own, but rather through the desire of Edward VI to secure a Protestant succession to the throne. After a brief reign of only nine days, she was displaced by Queen Mary. Even then, it is doubtful that she would have been executed except that members of her family continued to interfere in politics to her undoing. At length Queen Mary ordered the execution. The prayer book which she carried to the scaffold was borrowed from Sir John Brydges and is now preserved in the British Museum. Lady Jane Grey was executed in her seventeenth year, after a reign of nine days, with a bravery that could be duplicated by few men and surpassed by none.

Queen Mary I, in her reign of five years from 1553 to 1558, has left a few bindings, three of which are in the British Museum. These seem to have been designed by Berthelet, and are in brown calf with ornaments in gold arabesques, interlaced geometrical designs and scrollwork. The design and execution of these later bindings from the shop of Berthelet are far superior to the earlier ones done for Henry VIII.

The bindings of Queen Elizabeth are more numerous and the styles more diversified. Bindings in enameled gold, embroidered velvet and leather are to be found in her collection. The leather bindings frequently show examples of inlaid leathers of various colors and sunken panels are also employed. Fletcher reproduces a magnificent binding in dark olive morocco with a border of gold and blind tooling. Ornamental corners are of inlaid white leather stamped in gold. A bold scrollwork design of arabesques outlines a sunken panel in the center of each cover. This sunken panel contains the arms of the queen painted in colors on a ground of silver. Each side is decorated with four Tudor roses in silver, ensigned with crowns in gold. Some of her bindings in brown calf have the device of a crowned falcon holding a sceptre. This emblem originally belonged to Anne Boleyn but was continued by her daughter.

A binding on which the falcon appears is that covering a copy of the *Trogi Pompeii Historiarum Philippicarum Epitoma.* Although most of the bindings of this queen carry her initials, this example has only the falcon in the center of the boards and a sprig of oak at each of the four corners. The whole is enclosed in a border of a single rule with an ornament at each of the corners.

Some excellent bindings were done in Scotland at the end of the sixteenth century. Mary Queen of Scots has left us a few examples of this work, as has also James I. This king wrote for his son a curious book called *Basilicon Doron.* The original manuscript of this book is now in the British Museum beautifully bound. John Gibson was the appointed binder of the King of Scotland but, on his arrival in London, this office appears to have gone to John and Abraham Bateman. It is probable that the binding on the *Basilicon Doron* was done in Scotland by Gibson.

With the advent of James I, the Batemans became binders to the king, for the first time distinguishing the position of printer from that of binder, since all previous holders of this honor had been both printer and binder to the king. However, it is known that both Robert Barker, the king's Printer in Ordinary, and John Norton, the king's Printer for the Latin, Greek and Hebrew tongues, also bound books for the king. Norton seems to have bound mainly in velvets while Barker notes on his bills that books were bound in " Turkie leather, leather and vellum."

Books bound for James I generally have their sides powdered with various emblems. Some of these were doubtless executed by John and Abraham Bateman. Among the best of this style is a *Pontifical* and a *Ceremonial*. Both of these books are tooled with alternate vertical rows of thistles and fleurs-de-lis, with daisies interspersed. In the center of each cover are impressed the arms of the king. The back is treated in the same manner as the sides. The royal arms as they here appear contain the arms of Scotland and Ireland, surrounded with the garter and ensigned with the royal crown.

Two other books bound for King James I also command attention. The first of these is a presenta-

tion copy to the king of a copy of *Historiae Cante-
brigiensis Academiae.* This binding in brown calf
carries, in a heavy central panel, the Tudor rose,
which is crowned. Heavy cornerpieces depict mili-
tary trophies and the space between is decorated with
graceful gold tooling. The other binding is on the
*Plea Concerning the Bath and Bachelor Knights*
and is also in light brown calf. It has the arms in
the center and the field is powdered with fleurs-de-lis.
As is the case in so many of the bindings of this
king, the cornerpieces are exceedingly heavy and
detract from an otherwise admirable effect.

Henry, Prince of Wales, was also a great collector.
His books continue the use of large corner designs
such as the Tudor rose, crowned lions, or fleurs-de-lis.
The centerpiece almost invariably consists of his
arms. A delightful example of his bindings covers
a copy of *Livy* attractively bound in brown calf.
A light ornamental centerpiece encloses his badge in
gold and silver. On each side of the badge are his
initials. The border is composed of a single line
rule.

Charles, Prince of Wales, later Charles I, also had
an extensive collection. One of his bindings now in
the British Museum is in olive-brown morocco. The
covers, which bear his arms and initials, are decorated with graceful floriated tooling which is arabesque in character. The scrollwork in the bindings
of this king are suggestive of the work of the Eves
in France. A greater number of tools now appear

to be used on the English bindings, and these tools
are lighter in character than those previously employed. Although this tendency is entirely along
the lines of the French bindings, the examples cannot compare in beauty or execution with those of the
Continent.

Another design that is prevalent in English bookbinding of the seventeenth century is that in which
fan-shaped ornaments are prominent. This design
is an adaptation from the Italian bindings of the
early part of this century. It is made up of small
tools of mediocre design, being so placed in close
combination as to form a crowded central circular
ornament and semi-circular ones at the corners.

The bindings of the colony established by Nicholas
Ferrar at Little Gidding have been much discussed.
The examples known to exist are variously bound
in gilt-tooled leather, gilt-tooled velvet and red parchment. The most ornate copy is the *Harmony of the
Four Evangelists,* compiled for Charles I. It is a
large folio in blue leather which is lavishly decorated.
A broad-banded diamond panel contains a circle ornament surrounded by hearts. A segment of this
is repeated at each of the corners, and the whole field
contains a semis of small and large tools. Other
examples, more simply tooled, have single line rules
at half inch intervals, each panel having an ornament
at the angles.

During the Civil Wars and the period of the Commonwealth, bookbinding, along with every other ex-

pression of art, suffered and was allowed to die.  At
the Restoration, therefore, we find a different style
of bindings taking hold in England.  Francis Bow-
man appears to have regained his title as Stationer,
Bookseller and Bookbinder, but none of his bindings
have been traced.  At this time Samuel Mearne became Bookbinder to the King, receiving his grant
in June, 1660.  This position he filled according to the
accounts of the Great Wardrobe until 1683, when
Charles Mearne's name appears in the stead of
Samuel Mearne.

What appears to be one of the earlier books of
the elder Mearne is in the British Museum.  The
binding covers a *Book of Common Prayer* and is in
red morocco, each cover having a border of delicate
tooling enclosing a panel which is divided into three
compartments.  The central one contains the arms
of Charles II, and the upper and lower his cypher,
together with four doves, each of these doves being
ensigned with a crown and holding a palm branch in
its mouth.

Another binding by Samuel Mearne, now in the
British Museum, is probably the best example of
English bindings of the second half of the seventeenth
century.  It is in red morocco leather.  The covers
are adorned in what is termed the cottage pattern.
This name is applied because of the pent-like arrangement of lines at the top, bottom and sides.  In
this type the spaces are filled in with sprays and
branches combined with lacework, or with small

tools used in the fan ornament. Although the tools
which are used in these designs are often of inferior
quality, the bindings in their finished state are unusually attractive. The particular binding in question contains a center panel in which are impressed
the royal arms, and the design and execution of the
tools of which the binding is composed is of the finest
of the period.

Although this style in all probability was introduced from France, it is one of the few such patterns
that England was able to adapt to advantage. Several other bindings in the British Museum which
have been done in this style are credited to Samuel
Mearne.

The private libraries of England at this period
were neither very numerous nor very large. In a
letter to Samuel Pepys written in 1687, John Evelyn
says: " Paris alone, I am persuaded, is able to show
more [libraries] than all the three nations of Great
Britain." Evelyn, himself, had a fine collection,
many of his books having been done by Samuel
Mearne, in all probability.

Bindings from this period until the time of Roger
Payne show but little change in style. The successor
of Samuel Mearne employed his tools and followed
largely the cottage style, as did his contemporaries.
William Churchill and Edward Castle were the royal
binders from 1700 to 1755, and the British Museum
has many bindings of this period which they may
well have done. The earlier styles are, in general,

of better execution and design. Imitations of Le Gascon's manner may also be found at this time.

The Harleian style, alone of all this time, requires mention. It was a style attained under the patronage of Robert Harley, first Earl of Oxford, and by his son. This style, executed by the binders Eliot and Chapman, consisted of a broad-tooled border with center panels, in which the pineapple figures as a prominent tool.

Roger Payne learned his craft under Pote, the bookseller to Eton College. He established himself in London with the aid of Thomas Payne, a bookseller. Much of the work of Roger Payne is done in Russia leather, which had come into use about 1730. The balance was in straight grain morocco, either dark blue or bright red. His tools were original in form, being designed and engraved, it is said, by himself. They consisted of crescents, stars, leaves, acorns, running vines and circlets of gold, and were placed at intervals in the spaces to be decorated, the field being studded with gold dots. He was the first English binder who attempted to make his ornaments appropriate to the character of the book on which they were to be employed. At times, he has richly tooled the back of a volume to leave the sides almost entirely plain. His fine Russia work is partly blind-tooled and partly gilt, giving an effect that is unusually pleasing. All operations on the books bound by Payne are done with the greatest care.

# CHAPTER V

## BINDING IN AMERICA

THE HISTORY of the progress of bookbinding
on this side of the Atlantic has been almost
entirely lacking in literary exponents. In his *Bookbindings, Old and New,* Mr. Brander Matthews has
given some slighting comment on modern bookbinding in the United States and in other publications
similar, though generally shorter, remarks express
the author's attitude toward the progress of the art
in the New World. Some slight respect has been
shown the work of William Matthews in the realm
of book decoration but, in the main, its history in
America has been most notable through its absence.

In discussing this as well as other arts, it must be
recalled, as Daniel Berkley Updike expresses it in
his *Printing Types,* that " To make life beautiful was
not the motive that led to the settlement of New
England." Rather, therefore, than disregard the
efforts of the earlier American settlers in this branch
of art, their products should be considered with care
and with appreciation for the obstacles which they
had to overcome.

A survey of the bright and delicate bindings of
the seventeenth and eighteenth centuries in Europe
obviously is not an essential to an appreciative study

of bibliopegy in America where it could not be other than a tiresome struggle over a comparatively bleak and colorless field. The bindery in America was long but a necessary complement to the printing office. While it took time to develop in our midst a demand for artistic bookbinding, yet bookbinding has been carried on in the United States for a period of nearly three centuries, and the progress has often been more pronounced than might be expected. A study of this progress, therefore, should prove of interest at least to the American bibliophile.

One of the earliest examples of American bookbinding extant is that covering a copy of the third edition of the *Bay Psalm Book*. This book, which was printed in 1651, is more scarce than the first edition, only one copy being known. The book contains about 400 pages, 2½ x 4¼ inches in size. It is faultlessly bound in brown calf, the covers being held together with clasps of leather and brass. It is distinguished by but little ornament, a single gold line enclosing each cover and the initials F. B. appearing on either side of a small center ornament. This book was in the old Lenox collection which has since been incorporated in the New York Public Library.

A presentation copy of the same book, in the Prince revision of 1758, was also in this collection. Since this copy was presented to " The Honourable Thomas Hutchinson Esq., Lieut. Govr., etc., of The Province of the Massachusetts Bay in NE," it doubtless received very particular care in the binding, and may, even, have been done in England, although this is not supposed to have been the case. The binding is of red morocco with a thin gold line around the cover. Inside this line is a small panel marked out in gold lines with a thistle at each of the outer corners. The fact that more ordinary editions of this book are bound with the same tools, gives added strength to the claim that the binding was done in America. The Lenox collection also boasted a copy of this book in dark brown calf with exactly the same tooling.

As is so often the case in the craft of bookbinding, the earlier American binder very seldom placed his mark on his work. Our main knowledge of the names of binders is gathered from their printed notices appearing in the current newspapers. Since these binders were usually connected with printing offices, it is customary to find notices of which the following is an example from William Bradford's *Gazette:* "Printed and sold by William Bradford in New York where advertisements are taken in and where you may have old books, new Bound, either Plain or Gilt, and Money for Linen Rags." Similar notices appear in the *Philadelphia American Weekly Mercury* for Andrew Bradford, *The Maryland Gazette* for William Parks, and in many other eighteenth century publications.

Benjamin Franklin states that his paper is the "*Pennsylvania Gazette,* Printed by Benjamin Franklin, Post Master at the New Printing Office near the

Market, where advertisements are taken in and book-binding is done reasonably in the best manner." As an example of the "plain" bindings, we may mention a copy of *The Mohawk Prayer Book*, translated by Lawrence Claesse and printed by William Bradford, which is doubtless in its original binding of plain sprinkled sheep.

Although binding in America was generally carried on at the office of the printer, it may be interesting to note an advertisement in Bradford's *Gazette* of September, 1734, appearing for Joseph Johnson, and saying that " he is now set up Book-binding for himself as formerly, and lives in Duke St. (commonly called Bayard St.) near the Old-Slip Market; (New York) where all Persons in Town or Country, may have their Books carefully and neatly new Bound either Plain or Gilt reasonable."

A copy of Samuel Willard's *Body of Divinity* shows the tendency on the part of American binders to imitate as carefully as possible what they considered to be the accepted style in England. This book is bound in brown sheepskin with panel sides.

Isaiah Thomas, of Worcester, Mass., who was a true bibliophile as well as a printer, paper-maker, bookbinder and bookseller, advanced the art of the craft to some extent also through his writings. Although some of his " plain " bindings are still in service, the decorated panels, if he executed any such, have not existed to be put on record. Many of the *Chap Books* written and bound by this printer

were covered in a coarse and substantial brown
canvas or buckram, than which "there is nothing
cheaper, neater or more durable."

In Pennsylvania, the German settlers were founding their own types, printing and binding, as were the
English settlers of New England. The *Gesang Buch,*
printed at Germantown by Christopher Sauer, 2nd,
was bound plainly and solidly in brown calf with
brass knobs and brass-tipped leather clasps. The
sides have a panel in blind tooling with a modest
running border inside.

Bindings with borders in running patterns of gold
and sometimes containing a decorative panel in gold
continued to be produced through the eighteenth century. A copy of *The Contrast,* printed in Philadelphia in 1790, is bound in a highly polished dark red
morocco, the sides inlaid with green borders and with
ornamental gold tooling. Prior to the Revolution,
sheepskins and calfskins appear to have been the
only leathers used in American binding. After this
period, however, Russia came to be used to some
little extent and, much later, morocco came to be
the regularly accepted covering material for books
in de luxe bindings.

The earliest known book on bookbinding, pub-
lished in America, is that named *The Whole Art of
Book-binding, Containing Valuable Receipts for
Sprinkling, Marbling, Colouring, &c.* This is de-
scribed as being "the first American, from the third
London edition, with considerable additions" and

was published in Richmond by Peter Cottom, and "for sale at his law and miscellaneous Book-Store." The date of publication was 1824.

Another very early book on the subject of bookbinding in America was Edward Hazen's *The Panorama of Professions and Trades or Every Man's Book,* published in Philadelphia in 1837. This treatise covers the field with remarkable completeness, explaining the various operations and materials.

The advance made by America in bookbinding in the past fifty years needs no excuse. Although there are as yet few names which are outstanding in the field, those of William Matthews and his chief finisher, Frederick Gilson, cannot be omitted. The interest which at present is being shown by students in this work cannot pass without reward, and it is the support of the bibliophile which is most needed to bring this about.

During the nineteenth century bookbinding made rapid strides which are very evident, but much greater strides are to be made if the bestowal of the patronage of wealthy Americans is made among the many students of bookbinding in America.

# APPENDIX

# CONTEMPORANEOUS RULERS OF FRANCE AND ENGLAND

| FRANCE | ENGLAND |
|---|---|
| **15th CENTURY** | **15th CENTURY** |
| Charles VII, 1422 | Henry V, 1413 |
| Louis XI, 1461 | Henry VI, 1422 |
| Charles VIII, 1483 | Edward IV, 1461 |
| | Edward V, 1483 |
| Louis XII, 1498 { Jeanne, d. of Louis XI. Anne, Duchess of Brittany. | Richard III, 1483 |
| | Henry VII, 1485, Elizabeth, d. of Edward IV. |
| **16th CENTURY** | **16th CENTURY** |
| Francis I, 1515 { Claude, d. of Louis XII. Eleanor of Austria. | Henry VIII, 1509 { Katherine of Aragon. Anne Boleyn. Jane Seymour. Anne of Cleves. Catherine Howard. Catherine Parr. |
| Henry II, 1547, Catherine de Médicis. | |
| Francis II, 1559, Mary Stuart, Queen of Scotland. | |
| Charles IX, 1560, Regency of Catherine de Médicis. | |
| Henri, III, 1574, Louise de Vaudemont, called Louise de Lorraine. | |
| Henri IV, 1589 { Marguerite de Valois, d. of Henri II. Marie de Médicis. | Edward VI, 1547 Mary, 1553, Philip of Spain. Elizabeth, 1558 |

## 17th Century

Louis XIII, 1610, Anne of Austria, d. of Philip III of Spain.
Louis XIV, 1643, Maria Theresa, d. of Philip IV of Spain.

## 17th Century

James I, 1603, Anne of Denmark.
Charles I, 1625, Henrietta of France.
Commonwealth, 1649
Charles II, 1660, Catherine of Braganza.

James II, 1685 { Anne Hyde.
Marie Beatrice d'Este.

William and Mary, 1689
William III, 1694

## 18th Century

Louis XV, 1715, Mary Leczynska of Poland.
Philippe d'Orleans, grandson of Louis XIII, Regent 1715–1723.
Louis XVI, 1774, Marie Antoinette of Austria.
Louis XVII, 1793, never reigned.
Republic I, 1793–1799.

## 18th Century

Anne, 1702, Prince George of Denmark.
George I, 1714, Sophia Dorothea of Zell.
George II, 1727, Caroline of Anspach.
George III, 1760, Sophia Charlotte of Mecklenburg-Strelitz.

# CLASSICAL NAMES AND MODERN EQUIVALENTS

Being a list of the more important names of cities and towns used on the colophons and title-pages of old books, together with a corresponding list of the names now applied to these cities and towns.

*Abbatis Villa* — Abbeville
*Alabani Fanum* — St. Albans
*Ambianum* — Amiens (also *Samarobriva*)
*Antwerpia*}
*Anvers* } — Antwerp
*Aquæ Sextiæ* — Aix (also *Sestiæ*)
*Aquisgranum* — Aix-la-Chapelle (also *Urbs Aquensis*)
*Argentia* — Strassburg
*Arvernia* — Auvergne
*Augusta Tiberii* — Ratisbon
*Augusta Ubiorum* — Cologne (also *Colonia Agrippina*)
*Augusta Vindelicorum* — Augsburg
*Aurelia* — Orleans
*Avenio* — Avignon
*Basilea* — Basle
*Berma* — Bremen
*Bolonia* — Boulogne (also *Gesoriacum*)
*Bononia* — Bologna
*Borfusia* — Prussia
*Cæsarodunum* — Tours (also *Turones*)
*Cantabrigia* — Cambridge
*Cantuaria* — Canterbury (also *Durovernum*)

133

*Cestria* — Chester
*Colonia Agrippina* — Cologne (also *Augusta Ubiorum*)
*Divio* — Dion
*Duacum* — Douay
*Dublinum* — Dublin (also *Eblana*)
*Dunelmum* — Durham
*Durovernum* — Canterbury (also *Cantuaria*)
*Eblana* — Dublin (also *Dublinum*)
*Eboracum* — York
*Edinbruchium* ⎫
*Edinburgum* ⎬ — Edinburgh
*Exonia* — Exeter
*Gesoriacum* — Boulogne (also *Bolonia*)
*Glascua* — Glasgow
*Haga Comitum* — The Hague
*Lapurdum* — Bayonne
*Limovicum* — Limoges
*Lipsiæ* — Leipzig
*Londinium* ⎫
*Londinum* ⎬ — London
*Lotharingia* — Lorraine
*Lugduni* — Lyons
*Lugdunum Batavorum* — Leyden
*Lugdunum Segusianorum* — Lyons
*Lutetia* ⎫
*Lutetia Parisiorum* ⎬ — Paris
*Mancunium* — Manchester
*Massila* — Marseilles
*Mediolanum* — Milan
*Moguntiæ* ⎫
*Moguntiacum* ⎬ — Mayence
*Nicæa* — Nice
*Nordovicum* — Norwich
*Noriberga* ⎫
*Norica* ⎬ — Nuremberg

134

*Oxonia* — Oxford

*Padova*  
*Patavium* } — Padua

*Petriburgum* — Peterborough

*Remi* — Rheims

*Roffa* — Rochester

*Roma* — Rome

*Rothomagus* — Rouen

*Rupella* — Rochelle

*Samarobriva* — Amiens (also *Ambianum*)

*Sarum* — Salisbury

*Sena* — Sienna

*Sestiæ* — Aix (also *Aquæ Sextiæ*)

*Tridentum* — Trent

*Turones* — Tours (also *Cæsarodunum*)

*Urbs Aquensis* — Aix-la-Chapelle (also *Aquisgranum*)

*Varsovia* — Warsaw (also *Warsovia*)

*Venetiæ* — Venice (also *Vinegia*)

*Vestontio* — Besançon

*Vincentia* — Vincenza

*Vindobona* — Vienna

*Vinegio* — Venice (also *Venetiæ*)

*Warsovia* — Warsaw (also *Varsovia*)

*Westmonasterium* — Westminster

*Wintonia* — Winchester

*Wormacia* — Worms

# SELECT BIBLIOGRAPHY

Consisting of the more accessible of the books used for reference in preparing the present volume.

ANDREWS, W. L., Bibliopegy in the United States. *New York,* 1902.

BLADES, W., Books in Chains. *London,* 1892.

BRASSINGTON, W. S., Historic Bindings in the Bodleian Library. *London,* 1891.

COOKERELL, D., Bookbinding and the Care of Books. *London,* 1901.

CUNDALL, J., Bookbinding Ancient and Modern. *London,* 1891.

DAVENPORT, C., English Embroidered Bookbindings. *London,* 1899.

DAVENPORT, C., Royal English Bookbinding. *London,* 1897.

DAVENPORT, C., The Book: Its History and Development. *London,* 1907.

FLETCHER, W. Y., Bookbinding in France. *London,* 1894.

FLETCHER, W. Y., English Bookbindings in the British Museum. *London,* 1895.

FLETCHER, W. Y., Foreign Bookbindings in the British Museum. *London,* 1896.

GRUEL, L., Manuel de l'Amateur de Reliures. *Paris,* 1887.

HOE, R., One Hundred and Seventy-two Historic Bookbindings from the Library of Robert Hoe. *New York,* 1895.

HORNE, H. P., The Binding of Books. *London,* 1894.

# BIBLIOGRAPHY

MATHEWS, W., Modern Bookbinding Practically Considered. *New York, 1889.*

MICHEL, M., La Reliure Française. *Paris, 1881.*

PRIDEAUX, S. T., Historical Sketch of Bookbinding. *London, 1893.*

PRIDEAUX, S. T., Bookbinders and their Craft. *London, 1903.*

PRIDEAUX, S. T., Modern Bookbindings. *London, 1906.*

WEALE, W. H. J., Catalogue of Bookbindings . . . in the National Art Library, South Kensington. *London, 1894.*

WHEATLEY, H. B., Remarkable Bindings in the British Museum. *London, 1889.*

# INDEX

# INDEX